SERVING GOD

IN THE LOCAL CHURCH

Edition 2023

TATY OKUAN

WESTBOW
PRESS®
A DIVISION OF THOMAS NELSON
& ZONDERVAN

WestBow Press books may be ordered through booksellers or by contacting:

WestBow Press
A Division of Thomas Nelson & Zondervan
1663 Liberty Drive
Bloomington, IN 47403
www.westbowpress.com
844-714-3454

Unless otherwise indicated, all scripture quotations are taken from the New King James Version. Copyright © 1982 by Thomas Nelson, Inc. Used by permission. All rights reserved.

ISBN: 978-1-6642-9964-1 (sc)
ISBN: 978-1-6642-9965-8 (hc)
ISBN: 978-1-6642-9966-5 (e)

Library of Congress Control Number: 2023908684

Print information available on the last page.

WestBow Press rev. date: 7/5/2023

CONTENTS

DEDICATION

I dedicate this book to:

Anyone interested in Christianity and would like to learn more about the redemption in Jesus;

All Christians in the world, who love the Lord and would like to see His work expanding;

Anyone desiring to find a true Christian family in which to serve God with joy and love;

All pastors and church leaders who have experienced or are actually facing tough times in the exercise of their ministries, thus exposing their lives and families for the unique cause of the Gospel;

All my pastor friends and children in the faith, who are fighting the good fight of faith with me;

My beloved wife, Emmanuelle, and my treasured daughters Rachel, Tatiana, Kérène and Marie Rose OKUAN, along with my family members; I deeply love you all. May the grace and peace of God be our portion.

ACKNOWLEDGMENTS

First of all, I would like to thank my Redeemer and the Master of my life, the Lord Jesus Christ. To Him, I give thanks for the call to the pastoral and apostolic ministry He has given me. It is by His will that this book was written. I am grateful for His providence in my life.

My acknowledgments also go …

- To my dear wife Emmanuelle MULEKA, to whom I owe a deep consideration for the writing and full involvement in the elaboration of this work.
- To all my mentors, Bible school teachers and elders, for their unforgettable contributions in the shaping of my ministry;
- To my daughters, for their significant support during tough times in the ministry;
- To the whole community of Centre Évangélique
- "La Restauration," for their support and consideration;
- To my family, especially Cotine OKUAN, my elder sister
- for her encouragement;
- And to my Pastor friends, for their support and advice.

FOREWORD

For the more than thirty years that I have known Pastor Taty Okuan, it has always been in the service of the Lord. He was song leader, Choir member, Intercessor, English to French interpreter for me both in Nigeria and in many Churches as he accompanied me to preach the gospel of our Lord Jesus Christ both within and outside Nigeria. He has always lived his teaching in this book.

It is comforting to know that just as a child is born into a natural family to receive identity, be nurtured, reared, trained and prepared to face life ahead in a balanced manner, the church exists to provide the same for a child born into God's family. The local church is the spiritual family intended by God for the growth of every Christian. And just as every child identifies her role or is given a role to play within the family, and does so, the Christian/child of God should not be less engaged within the family framework of the church.

Pastor Taty Okuan, in this book, puts it succinctly that we are saved (born again) to serve, and stresses the importance of doing so in our local churches, bearing in mind the mission of the universal Church which are - evangelisation, edification and worship. He emphasises on the concept of servanthood and acceptable service to God as better enabled by discipleship and submission to the Holy Spirit who empowers us for ministry or service in His body.

He highlights the qualities of the kind of servant (worshipper) that God seeks as well as the pitfall to watch-out for and avoid in the life-long journey to serve, as God is looking for good and faithful servants, vessels of honour, useful to the Master. The kind that will trigger the manifestation of His power on this earth, those who do His will, not their own. God, who is the Builder of the Church, is Spirit, and needs us in order to materialise Himself. He wants to use our eyes, our hands, our feet and talents to accomplish His work. The question however, is, "Are we willing to do so?"

In this piece, Pastor Taty Okuan provides a manual that takes us through relationship between the believer, the local church and their responsibilities towards one another as intended by God, that should strike a genuine interest and hunger to do what pleases Him and ultimately, the preparation of the saints of God both for the harvest of souls and for the coming of the Lord!

This is a must read for every believer who truly wants to serve the Lord, it is a book for Church Leaders who want to build an Army of Loyal Workers, it is a text book for Bible Schools - for the training and equipping of Church Leaders.

Dr. Dare Olaoluwa.
Senior Pastor
Harvesting Faith Ministries
Lagos, Nigeria

PREFACE

In this book, the first of what I hope will be a series, Pastor Taty Okuan invites us to enter the doors of the sanctuary. With an experience of several decades working for the Lord, he shares with us the teachings received at the feet of the Master and collected here for the sake of His Church.

What he experienced and transmitted to his faithful children at the Centre Évangélique "La Restauration" of Ghent, the Church as a whole, can bene t from it today through this opus. Finding the importance of a locdevotedal church in this book, will also reveal to us the heart of a father, that of a shepherd who is always feeding and taking care of the herds, as well as urging them to the divine service; and that of the heavenly Father seeking to shape Christ in the hearts of His children.

The call of a local church is by then, nothing less than that of a family serving as an environment in which we are offered safety, and where the love surrounding our first steps in faith is assured. It is also the place where we learn how to serve the Lord according to His will such as was mentioned in the five-fold ministries. Consider then this invitation to serve, as a call from the One who said: "I am the way, the truth and the life." Pastor Mark MASY, a doulos of Christ[1]

---

[1] *Pastor Mark is theologian and professor of religion in Belgium*

INTRODUCTION

The main idea of this book came about as we were training the leaders of our community.

We came to realize that the people of God need to be educated about what the Lord is calling them to do, namely, to serve Him. This is exactly what God is looking for, from each believer. Yet, what should we understand by serving God? What does it imply? How do you proceed? Where do you do it?

From the concept of service, comes the importance of the place of service. There is a need to understand the role and the importance of being part of a local church in serving God. Why did the Lord establish the church for Christians? Why does the Lord recommend to each believer to belong to a specific community and never leave it? Should we serve God in a group or alone? What are God's expectations from each and every one of us, and more specifically, from us as it regards to our church?

The answers to all those questions are to be found in the Word of God, the Bible, which is nothing less than our preeminent reference. A good servant always seeks God's will and not that of man.

This book is intended to be one among many other thoughts on "the good servant" whom the Lord is looking for. It is an additional practical study for every Christian who desires to serve God by offering Him a marvelous service. The good servant serves God in his local church.

Presently, we are witnessing communities forgetting the importance of a local church. In other words, we are forgetting about the coordinated and effective service for God. In *Matthew 28:19*, Jesus gives His disciples the mission to "make disciples of all nations." This is the famous Great Commission given to the Church. We can see from the understanding of this directive issued by the Lord, that the priority lays on making disciples and not on simply winning souls, attending a congregation or multiplying seemingly "spiritual" activities.

It is important to understand that it is impossible to be a disciple without being a part of a local church to serve in. The notion of discipleship implies a stable relationship with one's instructors. Only a local congregational setting can provide this. The local church is important because it is our first actual Christian family. It is the place where we take our first steps in the faith; where our spiritual development starts. Its value should in no way be overlooked in our minds. The Lord speaks of destroying whoever wants to destroy His temple, whether it is our own body or His church.

This book is intended to address this topic that is so important to the spiritual growth of Christians: serving God and the importance of doing it in a local church. Together, we will see according to the Bible, some of the necessary qualities a good servant must develop. This teaching will help us progress on our path to maturity. We will also discuss the necessity of a local congregation, its organization, our service within it and our responsibility to watch over that sheepfold entrusted to us by God. We will better understand why it is important for every Christian to belong to a community, as urged in Hebrews 10:25: *not forsaking the assembling of ourselves together, as is the manner of some, but exhorting one another, and so much the more as you see the Day approaching.*

This book was written to contribute to the spiritual growth of all Christians and to the advancement of the Kingdom of God. We pray that you will enjoy the book and that it will help you reflect on your service to God!

May the Lord bless you!

Your Pastor, Taty Okuan
Senior Pastor
Centre Evangelique de la Restauration
Gentbrugge/Belgium

CHAPTER 1
SAVED TO SERVE

1

SAVED TO SERVE

I. SALVATION BY GRACE, NOT BY WORKS

There is no eternal life, without Christ. This is the message of salvation.

Man cannot reach the Lord by his own personal e orts, or by his good works. As it is impossible for a human being to live under water without a submarine, or to y without being in an airplane, it will be impossible for him to reach God, in other words, our good works do not grant us access to God. This is the reason why God sent His only begotten son, the Lord Jesus Christ, so that whoever believes in Him should not perish but have everlasting life (John 3:16). Jesus is the only way that leads to the Father, He is the truth and the life, the bridge between heaven and earth, between God and humanity.

It is impossible to live a life that pleases God if one has not received Christ as Savior and Lord. Christianity is not a religion or a set of dogmas that need to be applied. Christianity is based on, and begins with the revelation of the person of Christ and

His work concluded on the Cross for humanity. The Bible teaches us that the whole world is subject to sin.

1 John 5:19 "We know that we are of God, and the whole world lies under the sway of the wicked one."

As Tertullian said, you are not born a Christian, you become a Christian one day, even if you grew up in a Christian family and received a Christian education. Jesus told Nicodemus in John 3 "you must be born again" to be granted eternal life. It is interesting to note that Nicodemus was a good man and that he was respected within his society. Nicodemus was a doctor of the law, a Jew, a Pharisee, a member of the Sanhedrin, rich and well liked by all. But, in spite of all these good works, Christ tells him that he must be born again to have eternal life. Therefore, being well-integrated and well- renowned in society does not give us access to the presence of God. We must rst receive the One who is the way, that is, the person of Jesus Christ Himself. It is up to Man to personally seize the redemptive work accomplished by the Lord.

II. HOW TO BE BORN-AGAIN

Romans 10:9-10 says, That if you confess with your mouth the Lord Jesus and believe in your heart that God has raised Him from the dead, you will be saved. 10 For with the heart one believes unto righteousness, and with the mouth confession is made unto salvation. The Lord therefore comes to rescue the sinful man, fallen from His presence, to give him His life, "Zoe" (eternal life, the kind of life of God) as soon as he receives Him.

God does not force anyone and only acts according to the will of man. He will therefore wait until he (man) personally invites Him into his heart.

Revelation 3:20 "*Behold, I stand at the door and knock. If anyone hears My voice and opens the door, I will come in to him and dine with him, and he with Me.*"

Man must therefore make a personal covenant with God. He makes a pact with the Lord so that He may come and dwell in his heart. To do this, one must first of all believe that Jesus died for one's own sins, recognize that He rose from the dead, and then decide to follow him. It is then necessary that one confesses this faith publicly with his mouth, by receiving Jesus Christ as Savior and Lord.

If reading this text, you feel concerned about this and you wish to receive Jesus Christ as Lord and Savior, we invite you to do so now. You can confess it either in front of a Christian witness or at a nearby church. You can also contact the "Centre Évangélique De La Restauration" church (Facebook: Centre Évangélique De La Restauration) and profess this covenant prayer aloud:

"Lord Jesus Christ, here I am, coming to You. I recognize that You died on the Cross for my sins and I decide to follow You. Forgive my sins. I invite You into my heart. I believe that You died and rose again, that You are the Son of God, the only way that leads us to the Father. I receive You today as Lord and Savior of my life. Give me Your life and guide me. Amen."

We are then saved. We are from now on, members of God's family! From that day the Lord gives His Holy Spirit to man in order to guide him on how to live the life designed by God; to serve him. The Lord gives us His Word – the Bible, to instruct us.

Furthermore, man lives his entire life as worship unto God.

III. COMMANDMENT OF SERVICE

After having received Jesus as Lord and Savior, we are saved. It means that, from a spiritual standpoint, we have left behind the world in order to serve the Lord. We are not saved just to be saved. That doesn't make any sense. We are saved for the purpose of living God's life, serving Him, and manifesting God on earth. We were created to worship the Lord, to glorify Him and to work for Him.

Away from salvation, we cannot pretend to serve according to God's will. It is only when we are born again that the Lord places His Spirit and nature in us. The man having the Spirit of God in him, is thus enlightened and can walk in His light; Ephesians 1:13 In Him you also trusted, after you heard the word of truth, the gospel of your salvation; in whom also, having believed, you were sealed with the Holy Spirit of promise,

The divine commandment of service according to God is beforehand to receive Christ as Lord and Savior. He is the cornerstone, the one who enables us to produce. Then, on this same foundation will come the good works according to God, that is, the service and the worship that we offer to the Lord.

Let us not put the cart before the horse by reversing this order! We are first of all saved to serve. We do not serve to be saved. And we cannot serve God without having been initially saved by Him. This is the principle of the "New Birth": the child is born as a baby, then progressively grows by being nourished and benefitting from the care of his parents; from the family environment. The same is applicable in the spiritual domain.

It is God who gives us birth in spirit. Man cannot give birth to Himself .

Since the fall of Adam, sin has entered the world. The human race has since been separated from God. It is therefore impossible for us to have access to the divine presence of God. The natural man (who does not have the Spirit of God) lives his life without God, in his own way and is a slave to sin.

Romans 3:23 *"for all have sinned and fall short of the glory of God ."*

1 Corinthians 2:14-15 *"But the natural man does not receive the things of the Spirit of God, for they are foolishness to him; nor can he know them, because they are spiritually discerned. 15 But he who is spiritual judges all things, yet he himself is rightly judged by no one."*

God told Moses to go and tell Pharaoh to let His people go so that they could serve Him! Given that it is impossible for man to give by Himself the worship due to God, through Christ he has obtained the ability to overcome the world. He has received the Holy Spirit who enlightens him and that is why the Lord recommends us to "walk according to the Spirit,," so that we will not satisfy the desires of the flesh. Having received the Spirit and the Bible, we can therefore go forward in serving God according to His will.

And the Lord wants us to be good servants. We will therefore have to learn to consider His Word to develop the qualities of a good worker. Of course, not all Christians have been called into the five-fold ministry (Apostle, Evangelist, Prophet, Pastor and Teacher).

But, we have all received some particular gifts and particular callings. Everyone serves God following his vocation. This may apply in the secular, physical, intellectual or spiritual fields.

In any case, it is up to every Christian, even those working in the secular field, to have a fixed local church in which to serve God faithfully. Man is not only a physical or psychic being, he is also a spiritual being. Every Christian must therefore preserve his relationship with God, the same relationship that will have an impact in all aspects of his life.

IV. THE CHRISTIAN FAMILY

In saving us, God gives us a concrete and fixed Christian family. This is the local church. Its role is to ensure our spiritual growth. Within, we do have some rights as members.

Any growth always requires a good structure. Without a structure or a family, it is impossible to properly grow. The church is nothing else than that spiritual family that will allow a Christian to know God more and finally reach his destiny. A Christian who is only interested in claiming his new birth, without serving God in a real congregation, is not following the will of the Lord and may return to his old life in the world.

1 Peter 4:10. *"As each one has received a gift, minister it to one another, as good stewards of the manifold grace of God."*

Acts 2:41-42 *"Then those who gladly received his word were baptized; and that day about three thousand souls were added to them. 42 And they continued steadfastly in the apostles' doctrine and fellowship, in the breaking of bread, and in prayers."*

After having listened to the preaching of the Apostle Peter, the first

Christians persevered in the 4 pillars which are: the teaching of the Apostles, fellowship, prayers and the breaking of bread. These are the four essential, basic principles for growing in faith. This verses from the book of Acts show us that believers have persevered in the practice of these 4 principles. The word "persevere" means that they had to make e orts despite external or internal opposition in obeying God's will.

Fellowship, teachings and community prayers belong within the framework of the local assembly. Spiritual growth can therefore not take place outside the church. The local church is this sheepfold chosen by God, necessary for the personal growth of every man, because it provides care and spiritual provision and allows the exercise of the duties to be fulfilled.

We cannot pretend to be disciples of Jesus without a real local church to which we belong, and in which we put the gifts we have received at the service of others. The Lord does not want us to be "jobless." Let us serve God with our talents. We are saved to be trained and to serve. God places us in a family that will build us up. Each of us is a stone in the building. Every Christian is a member of the body of Christ. Without that member, the body will not work properly.

1 Peter 2:5 *"You also, as living stones, are being built up a spiritual house, a holy priesthood, to offer up spiritual sacrifices acceptable to God through Jesus Christ."*

V. 5. SOME ADVICE FOR THE CHRISTIAN WALK

Beloved, we urge you to belong to a good and fixed local church that is led by a good pastor, who is himself subject to the Holy Spirit and the Word of God. Perhaps, you have recently received Jesus as Lord and Savior and do not know which church to attend. It is up to you to pray to the Lord to find an assembly where the Word of God is the cornerstone of that assembly.

We must warn you that there are many misleading people, who are not real men of God, but who however, like to gather people for all kinds of prayers by promising miracles and prayers for wealth. Do not give in to the charms of this kind of gathering, and please, verify first if the shepherd of this assembly is trained enough to teach the Word of God; in other words, to ensure your spiritual growth. If not the case, pray to the Lord to guide you in finding a church.

The Holy Spirit will guide you.

Perhaps, you find yourself in a situation where you no longer have a local assembly because, justified or not, you feel disappointed. If that is the case, we recommend you to get up and pray to the Lord to direct you toward a local church, for, it is His will that you be part of an assembly. You may have faced the "so-called pastors" who did not fear God. Remember, not all shepherds are like that. Remember the story of the prophet, Elijah. At his time, the people of Israel were going through a profound spiritual decline. Elijah thought he was the only remaining faithful to God. This was totally false! So let us not be pessimistic. The Lord told Elijah that there are still 7000 men who serve Him, and who have not bowed their knees before Baal!

This is the same case today.

1 Kings 19:18 " ...*Yet I have reserved seven thousand in Israel, all whose knees have not bowed to Baal, and every mouth that has not kissed him.*"

Beloved in the Lord, you are valuable, you are a member of the body of Christ. Do not let this potential of gifts and talents be buried. Serve God correctly. God always blesses service. Do not let any negativity influence you. The brothers and sisters in the faith are a blessing to you. They will help your gifts to unfold. The local church plays a big role in this. Continue your walk with God. The Lord will bless you. The Bible says that He is the Rewarder of those who seek Him. Let us not forget that we are saved to serve! To serve is to worship God! Keep serving God. Never stop doing so and above all, do it according to His will.

CHAPTER 2
FAITHFULNESS

2

FAITHFULNESS

I. A PROPER SERVICE

God created man and placed in each of us specific talents, making each one of us unique. We were created to live for God and are called to render our service to Him, each according to his or her vocation. Every Christian is therefore a servant of God, each following his or her calling, whether in the ecclesiastical or secular sphere. The Lord is looking for good servants. Hence, we must offer him a proper service.

So, what is a proper service according to God?

When we talk about service, we tend to focus primarily on the aspect of skills, efficiency and result to be obtained, rather than on the intrinsic nature of the offered service. The Bible tells us that man looks on the outward appearance, but God looks at the heart. The heart is the source of life.

The secular world, especially in the West, demands more and more that we prove our skills. For example, if you want to get hired for the job you are applying for, you need to know how to show yourself o . You need to show o your skills. If you fail to do so, even if you are skilled enough, you will have a hard time getting that job. These habits of life can have an influence on our way of understanding service according to God.

We tend to be attracted by the charisma of a preacher rather than by his nature or his character. For example, we may lay more emphasis on the preacher's ability to communicate, his dynamism, his ability to touch people's hearts, etc. We are therefore tempted to emphasize the outer, rather than the inner qualities of man. We focus more on the know-how than on the being himself.

But, before performance, comes the being. The being is the most important. God is first interested in our inner being. If this is good, the resulting service will be positively influenced. Yes, developing skills is important and you should strive to do it. But this is not crucial! The first quality required to be a good servant of God is faithfulness!.

You cannot trust a competent, but unfaithful person. You cannot build a strong relationship with an unfaithful partner. Soon or later, they will betray you and your business or marriage would not be moving forward. They will embezzle money from your company, they will destroy the relationships with their partner, friends, etc., because they are too self-centered.

It is a mistake to marry someone who is physically attractive, but unfaithful.

It is a mistake to trust a charismatic, but unfaithful Pastor.

It is a mistake to ordain a charismatic, but unfaithful deacon. A faithful person, even if he lacks competence, is useful. He will be able to develop his strength over time.

Proverbs 20:6 *"Most men will proclaim each his own goodness, But who can find a faithful man? "*

Faithfulness to His Word is the first quality God looks for in His servants. It is all about being attached to His person, being devoted to Him, being constant and persevering in the face of opposition .

Despite the fact that He is sovereign, God never acts without going through men. This is why He is absolutely looking for faithful men who will faithfully transmit His message, accomplish His will and not their own. Unfortunately, rare is this type of people needed by God. May we develop this precious quality and maintain it until the return of our Lord Jesus Christ!

Jeremiah 5:1 *"Run to and fro through the streets of Jerusalem; See now and know; And seek in her open places If you can find a man, If there is anyone who executes [a] judgment, Who seeks the truth, And I will pardon her."*

Psalms 89:20-21 *" I have found My servant David; With My holy oil I have anointed him, 21. With whom My hand shall be established; Also My arm shall strengthen him."*

Isaiah 42:1-4 *"Behold! My Servant whom I uphold, My Elect One in whom My soul delights! I have put My Spirit upon Him; He will bring forth justice to the Gentiles. 2 He will not cry out, nor raise His voice, Nor cause His voice to be heard in the street. 3 A bruised reed*

He will not break, And smoking flax He will not quench; He will bring forth justice for truth. 4 He will not fail nor be discouraged, Till He has established justice in the earth; And the coastlands shall wait for His law."

II. THE "DOULOS" SERVANT

The Lord is therefore looking for faithful servants in order to transcribe His will and not theirs. This requires man to develop humility.

Nowadays, we see a certain tendency in our Christian circles, to desire at all costs, to occupy high ecclesiastical functions. Some people believe that becoming a Pastor, an Apostle, more commonly known as a "servant of God," allows them to acquire a high social status. They hope to be respected and to gain different kinds of honors. This reasoning is dangerous and unbiblical. And this will push man not only to destroy his fellow man, but also the work of God.

Acquiring positions in the church should not be seen as a promotion, but as a great responsibility. Because, the more the Lord continues to assign tasks, the more you must listen to Him in order to do His will and not yours. The more responsibilities you get, the more you must learn to be humble, to sacrifice yourself, to lose, to give up, to suffer, to put to death your fleshly nature.

The notion of "servant of God" according to the world is carnal. It greatly differs from the "servant of God" according to God. The word servant in the Bible is "doulos" in ancient Greek. This is the type of servant that the Lord is looking for.

1. We are all "doulos" for God. But what is a "doulos?"

The Ancient Greek has several variations, but the root of this word remains the same and means *servant, slave*. *"Doulos"*[2] is therefore this servant who is dependent on the master, the one who is at the service of a superior. But beware, this is not a slave forced to be a slave! A doulos servant is a person who, without being forced or pressured to do so, voluntarily puts himself at the service of a superior.

We find this idea of *"doulos"* in *Exodus 21:5-6*, *"But if the servant plainly says, 'I love my master, my wife, and my children; I will not go out free,' 6 then his master shall bring him to the judges. He shall also bring him to the door, or to the doorpost, and his master shall pierce his ear with an awl, and he shall serve him forever."*

This verse shows us the notion of the decision of a man's free will to become someone's servant, to be devoted to him.

2. What the "doulos" concept is not:

2.1. Doulos is not involuntary enslavement or the result of insufficiency

The concept of *"doulos,"* which according to *Exodus 21:5-6*, means servant or slave, may at the first glimpse concern us, taking into account the ideas of our time. Indeed, slavery is known to us as being constraining and destroying the personality and the future of the victim. It is important to

---

[2] *The information taken from commentary of the Bible, louis segond version, comments by John MacArthur*

analyze the concept of *doulos* according to its historical context in order to understand what this notion really implies.

The law in Israel at the time of the Exodus compared to the various civil codes of the ancient Near East used to regulate slavery. Slavery for economic or any other reason was supposed to last only six years at most. Beyond this period of time, slavery had to end unless the slave himself chose to remain in the service of his master, in a context of love and not of abuse. Any permanent and involuntary enslavement of a Hebrew in the service of another Hebrew was at that time undesirable in the Israelite society. At this stage, the man could accept to become a slave, not for economic reasons, or for lack of something, but by love and attachment towards his master for whom he was willing to o er his services.

The "doulos" servant is a person passionate about the cause, which is the vision of another person whom he considers an example to follow and whom he wants to serve.

Deuteronomy 15:16-17 *"And if it happens that he says to you, 'I will not go away from you,' because he loves you and your house since he prospers with you, 17 then you shall take an awl and thrust it through his ear to the door, and he shall be your servant forever. Also to your female servant you shall do likewise."*

2.2. The "doulos" concept is different from the Suzerainty Covenant in the Middle Ages

"The Suzerainty[3] Covenant" was established by a powerful Suzerain (lord, king,) in favor of a weaker and dependent

---

[3] *Note of the hermeneutics course of professor David Remy of the CTS year 2020-2021*

vassal (the defeated, subjected people). It guaranteed the vassal protection and certain benefits, but in return, the vassal was required to show exclusive loyalty to the suzerain. And he was warned that any disloyalty (infidelity) would result in the punishments specified in the covenant. To show his loyalty, the vassal would observe the terms (rules of conduct, laws) specified in the covenant. As long as the vassal was respecting the terms, the suzerain knew he was loyal. For any mistake, punitive measures were taken. Our relationship with God is not like that. It consists of free will and it is based on love. God is Father. No matter what, the Lord remains the Creator of men, even men who do not want a relationship with Him as Father.

2.3. The "doulos" concept is different from the modern forms of slavery

By virtue of the definition given in the first point of this chapter, the "doulos" concept is therefore also different from the modern forms of slavery. It is not a situation[8] where one is forced to serve another by being deprived of his rights and freedom.

2.4. The "doulos" concept is different from the modern employment

The "doulos" concept is also different from the notion of service and employment contract of our modern time, where a worker commits himself to an employer, to perform work in return for payment.

3. Service According To God

God created man to glorify Him, to worship Him and to serve Him, in return. The Bible shows us that all creation was made for the sole purpose of worshiping God. We were therefore, created to serve the Lord. This is God's original plan for man, these are His designs for us.

Isaiah 43:21 This people I have formed for Myself; They shall declare My praise.

Ephesians 2:10 "For we are His workmanship, created in Christ Jesus for good works, which God prepared beforehand that we should walk in them."

Man is called to serve not man, the earth or creation, but God, the Creator of all things. By serving God, both men and the creation bene t from the service rendered. As a matter of fact, man is not the "doulos" (the servant) of any man or any other creature. He is only a "doulos" to God. Man's true happiness is found in the exercise of God's will. The attraction to sin will never give us true happiness.

Bible says in *Jeremiah 29:11 "that God has a good plan for us "For I know the plans I have for you," declares the Lord, "plans to prosper you and not to harm you, plans to give you hope and a future."NIV*

When Adam and Eve sinned in Genesis by wanting to fulfill their own will, and not God's, sin entered the world. Thus, man was left to himself, alone in his walk without God. He had become a slave to sin.

Man is corrupted, hence, his service is also corrupted because he wants to fulfill himself rather than serve. This ideology leads man towards objectification and the domination of his fellow man and all creation. The work of Christ accomplished on the Cross aims to make us servants ("doulos") of God according to the will of the Creator.

4. The Christ, Our Example Of Excellence

The Lord Jesus Christ was Himself the faithful servant of excellence. He serves as an example of the service that God expects from us. Here, we have two Bible verses that show us this well : *Matthew 20:28*, "just as the Son of Man did not come to be served, but to serve, and to give His life a ransom for many."

Philippians 2:5-8 "*Let this mind be in you which was also in Christ Jesus, 6 who, being in the form of God, did not consider it robbery to be equal with God, 7 but made Himself of no reputation, taking the form of a bondservant, and coming in the likeness of men. 8 And being found in appearance as a man, He humbled Himself and became obedient to the point of death, even the death of the cross.*"

5. How to develop the exercise of one's service for God

The notion of the "doulos" servant concept means that man no longer does his own will, nor the will of a man, but that of God. In order to be able to do this, he must, first of all, develop his ability to listen to the Lord before acting. In order to understand God, grasp His will and be able to execute it, it is important for a man to have a personal and daily prayer life, a life of intimacy with the Lord, and of meditation on His Word. If these principles are not applied, man will sink into activism, instead of serving God. Activism is the act of serving according to man's conception of things. The consequence is posing actions that are neither spiritual nor productive.

The slave (doulos) described in Exodus 21, who voluntarily wanted to remain working with his master, automatically had to have his ear pierced. It was a sign of his submission and belonging to his lord. This act symbolized his ability to listen. By listening, an intimate relationship is established and the servant can do the will of the Lord. It is easier to understand and obey someone we already know, rather than someone we do not.

Isaiah 50:4 *"The Lord God has given Me The tongue of the learned, That I should know how to speak A word in season to him who is weary. He awakens Me morning by morning, He awakens My ear To hear as the learned."*

Let us take Mary (one of the sisters of Lazarus, the man Jesus raised from the dead) as an example. She was attentive when Jesus came to visit them. She preferred to listen to Jesus rather than being busy like her sister, Martha, with multiple domestic tasks (that is, with multiple unnecessary activities that meet the expectations of men). It is only by being at the feet of the Master that one can understand His will and carry it out. And only by this will we then be able to give God an effective and pleasing service that will be a blessing to those around us.

Luke 10:41-42 *"And Jesus answered and said to her, "Martha, Martha, you are worried and troubled about many things. 42 But one thing is needed, and Mary has chosen that good part, which will not be taken away from her."*

It is through his intimacy with God that man learns to conform to His will in order to faithfully serve Him. This requires a life of total dedication and obedience.

6. Selecting collaborators in the church

The work of God is carried out and grows through loyal workers, who allow themselves to be trained by God, by developing their abilities, and finally, be sent to the work field. These are servants that really understand the demands of the commitment they have made. And this applies even more to those who are called to occupy ecclesiastical positions.

Exodus 18:21 *"Moreover you shall select from all the people able men, such as fear God, men of truth, hating covetousness; and place such over them to be rulers of thousands, rulers of hundreds, rulers of fifties, and rulers of tens."*

Acts 6:3 *"Therefore, brethren, seek out from among you seven men of good reputation, full of the Holy Spirit and wisdom, whom we may appoint over this business;"*

Deuteronomy 1:13 *"Choose wise, understanding, and knowledgeable men from among your tribes, and I will make them heads over you."*

Proverbs 20:25 *"It is a trap for a man to [speak a vow of consecration and] say rashly, "It is holy!" And [not until] afterward consider [whether he can fulfill it]."* (AMP Version)

III. SOME CHARACTERISTICS OF A GOOD SERVANT

A servant of God must therefore remain faithful and keep developing his skills in order to perform a proper service before God. He must add several virtues to his faith.

In this chapter, we will identify 9 qualities[4] that allow us to be good servants. All these virtues will be added to the one which is considered the foundation of all: faithfulness!

1. Worker

A good servant must be hardworking.
If we really want to serve God, we must fight against laziness. Lazy people are always looking for the easiest way. But, nothing is easy under the sun. People should not work completely relying on what they feel inspired to do. A good service is made of only 5% of inspiration and the other 95% is hard work. A servant must therefore work on his prayer life, his reading of the Word, his character, his sermon, his relationships with men, his relationship with God, his skills, his values, his studies, his technique, etcetera. As the parable of talents in Matthew 25 explains to us, we are called to multiply the talent that God has given us.

Matthew 25:16-30 "Then he who had received the five talents went and traded with them, and made another five talents. 17 And likewise he who had received two gained two more also. 18 But he who had received one went and dug in the ground, and hid his lord's money. 19 After a long time the lord of those servants came and settled accounts with them. 20 "So he who had received five talents came and brought

---

[4] *Inspired by W.Nee's book « the true servant of God"*

five other talents, saying, 'Lord, you delivered to me five talents; look, I have gained five more talents besides them.' 21 His lord said to him, 'Well done, good and faithful servant; you were faithful over a few things, I will make you ruler over many things. Enter into the joy of your lord.' 22 He also who had received two talents came and said, 'Lord, you delivered to me two talents; look, I have gained two more talents besides them.' 23 His lord said to him, 'Well done, good and faithful servant; you have been faithful over a few things, I will make you ruler over many things. Enter into the joy of your lord.' 24 "Then he who had received the one talent came and said, 'Lord, I knew you to be a hard man, reaping where you have not sown, and gathering where you have not scattered seed. 25 And I was afraid, and went and hid your talent in the ground. Look, there you have what is yours.' 26 "But his lord answered and said to him, 'You wicked and lazy servant, you knew that I reap where I have not sown, and gather where I have not scattered seed. 27 So you ought to have deposited my money with the bankers, and at my coming, I would have received back my own with interest. 28 So take the talent from him and give it to him who has ten talents. 29 'For to everyone who has, more will be given, and he will have abundance; but from him who does not have, even what he has will be taken away. 30 And cast the unprofitable servant into the outer darkness. There will be weeping and gnashing of teeth. »

2 Timothy 4:2 "Preach the word! Be ready in season and out of season. Convince, rebuke, exhort, with all longsuffering and teaching."

2 Peter 1:5-9 "But also for this very reason, giving all diligence, add to your faith virtue, to virtue knowledge, 6 to knowledge self-control, to self-control perseverance, to perseverance godliness, 7 to godliness brotherly kindness, and to brotherly kindness love. 8 For if these things are yours and abound, you will be neither barren nor unfruitful in the knowledge of our Lord Jesus Christ. 9 For he who lacks these things is shortsighted, even to blindness, and has forgotten that he was cleansed from his old sins."

John 5:17 *"But Jesus answered them, "My Father has been working until now, and I have been working."*

John 4:35 *"Do you not say, 'There are still four months and then comes the harvest'? Behold, I say to you, lift up your eyes and look at the fields, for they are already white for harvest!*

All these verses show us the eagerness that we must have in the execution of the work that is asked of us. We absolutely have to avoid laziness!"

2. Stability

A servant of God is required to always be in a state of mental stability while facing his responsibilities. He must avoid changing his mind or his commitments in the face of di cult circumstances. He must develop enough maturity to do his job. Otherwise, he will not inspire confidence.

Proverbs 25:28 *"Whoever has no rule over his own spirit Is like a city broken down, without walls."*

1 Peter 2:5 *"you also, as living stones, are being built up a spiritual house, a holy priesthood, to offer up spiritual sacrifices acceptable to God through Jesus Christ."*

Looking into the life of the Apostle Peter, we see that his mind was wavering and unstable for a very long time. He had to learn how to build his personality before being powerfully used by the Holy Spirit. The Gospels show us how, after receiving revelation that Jesus is the Christ, Peter immediately was used by the devil. He then tried to dissuade Jesus from accomplishing His mission of dying on the Cross to save sinners. And when Jesus was arrested, we see him denying the Lord three times in front of a woman!

Matthew 16: 13-23 *"When Jesus came into the region of Caesarea Philippi, He asked His disciples, saying, "Who do men say that I, the Son of Man, am?" 14 So they said, "Some say John the Baptist, some Elijah, and others Jeremiah or one of the prophets." 15 He said to them, "But who do you say that I am?" 16 Simon Peter answered and said, "You are the Christ, the Son of the living God." 17 Jesus answered and said to him, "Blessed are you, Simon Bar-Jonah, for flesh and blood has not revealed this to you, but My Father who is in heaven. 18 And I also say to you that you are Peter, and on this rock I will build My church, and the gates of Hades shall not prevail against it. 19 And I will give you the keys of the kingdom of heaven, and whatever you bind on earth will be bound in heaven, and whatever you loose on earth will be loosed in heaven." 20 Then He commanded His disciples that they should tell no one that He was Jesus the Christ. 21 From that time Jesus began to show to His disciples that He must go to Jerusalem, and suffer many things from the elders and chief priests and scribes, and be killed, and be raised the third day. 22 Then Peter took Him aside and began to rebuke Him, saying, "Far be it from You, Lord; this shall not happen to You!" 23 But He turned and said to Peter, "Get behind Me, Satan! You are [d] an offense to Me, for you are not mindful of the things of God, but the things of men."*

Mark 14:54 and 66-72 *"But Peter followed Him at a distance, right into the courtyard of the high priest. And he sat with the servants and warmed himself at the fire. 66 Now as Peter was below in the courtyard, one of the servant girls of the high priest came. 67 And when she saw Peter warming himself, she looked at him and said, "You also were with Jesus of Nazareth." 68 But he denied it, saying, "I neither know nor understand what you are saying." And he went out on the porch, and a rooster crowed. 69 And the servant girl saw him again, and began to say to those who stood by, "This is one of them." 70 But he denied it again. And a little later those who stood by said to Peter again, "Surely you are one of them; for you are a Galilean, and your speech shows it." 71 Then he began to curse and swear, "I do not know this Man of whom you speak!" 72 A second time the rooster crowed. Then Peter called to mind the word that Jesus had said to him, "Before the rooster crows twice, you will deny Me three times." And when he thought about it, he wept."*

3. Loving all people

The servant of God must love everyone. He must not show any kind of favoritism in his relationships with others. He must be able to live in harmony with himself and society. To do so, he must get mature enough to respect and acknowledge the differences and limitations of each person.

To love is to help one's brothers and sisters, support them, and forgive them. However, one does not have to develop a friendship or familiarity with everyone. Just as God gives sunshine and rain to everyone without being the Father of all, we cannot be friends with everyone either.

As God loves man, we are also commanded to love everyone. Note that Jesus Himself preferred to be called "son of man" rather than "son of God." In the New Testament, the title "son of man" is mentioned 83 times when Jesus speaks of Himself.

Man is truly at the heart of His mission of salvation. Let us, therefore, have sympathy for lost souls. Let us not judge them or look down on them. Let us not forget our own past. We were all sinners like them. The Lord used people who showed us love, who were patient with us, and who taught us. And today, we have become servants of God. We must have this same attitude towards those who live in sin away from the Lord.

Let us, rst of all, understand the verse "God created man" in order to be equipped to start preaching the Word of God to that lost soul. *John 3:16* says, *For God so loved the world that He gave His only begotten Son, that whoever believes in Him should not perish but have everlasting life.*

Mark 10:45; " For even the Son of Man did not come to be served, but to serve, and to give his life as a ransom for many."

Luke 19:10; "For the Son of Man has come to seek and to save that which was lost."

John 10:10 "The thief does not come except to steal, and to kill, and to destroy. I have come that they may have life and that they may have it more abundantly."

While writing to Timothy, a Pastor in Ephesus, the Apostle Paul is asking him to think of the authorities and all men without exception in his intercession.

1 Timothy 2:1-3 "Therefore I exhort first of all that supplications, prayers, intercessions, and giving of thanks be made for all men, 2 for kings and all who are in authority, that we may lead a quiet and peaceable life in all godliness and reverence. 3 For this is good and acceptable in the sight of God our Savior."

4. Knowing how to listen

A very important and powerful quality for a servant of God is listening. Knowing how to listen to God and knowing how to listen to men. For example, in an interview, more than half the problem is solved when you have listened and understood what a person intended to say.

Developing this quality is not easy. But, it is not impossible either. People with an impulsive attitude often find it quite di cult to develop this skill because listening requires calmness and patience. A servant, and especially a department head in a church, must be able to listen to what is being said to him, the meaning of what was said, what was not said, what was intended to be said, and to do all of these with love and without being suspicious. We must therefore pray for the Holy Spirit to give us this discernment.

You must first listen to the other in order to understand what the other person is saying in order to understand his or her thoughts, and at the same time, avoid adding your own opinions. You have to listen carefully to avoid giving the same remedy or the same solution to any problem that arises. We need to learn to be objective rather than having a judgment based on personal feelings.

There is a popular saying that says "the longer you listen, the more others move their lips and teeth."

Luke 2:46–47 *"Now so it was that after three days they found Him in the temple, sitting in the midst of the teachers, both listening to them and asking them questions. 47 And all who heard Him were astonished at His understanding and answers."*

The Greek word ἀκούω (akouô) means to listen, to hear. It is mentioned around 1440 times in the Septuagint[5], including 500 times in the New Testament. Listening, therefore, occupies a very special place in being able to serve God.

5. Know how to measure your words

The Scriptures show us that the tongue is a powerful instrument that communicates life or death. The tongue, although it has no bones, has the power to destroy a forest and the beings created by God. The servant of God must be mature enough to control his words.

Please note: We must know whom to con de in and whom to talk to and exchange ideas with, since the tongue is the exit door of our being. The Bible says that it is from the abundance of the heart (of the being) that the mouth (the tongue) speaks.

James 3:1-2; "My brethren, let not many of you become teachers, knowing that we shall receive a stricter judgment. 2 For we all stumble in many things. If anyone does not stumble in word, he is a [a] perfect man, able also to bridle the whole body."

Ecclesiastes 5:3; "For a dream comes through much activity, And a fool's voice is known by his many words."

1 Timothy 3:8; "Likewise deacons must be reverent, not double-tongued, not given to much wine, not greedy for money, …"

Matthew 5:36-37; "Nor shall you swear by your head, because you cannot make one hair white or black. 37 But let your 'Yes' be 'Yes,'

---

[5] *The Septuagint is a translation of the Hebrew Bible into Greek koine*

and your 'No,' 'No.' For whatever is more than these is from the evil one."

Ephesians 5:4; *"Neither filthiness, nor foolish talking, nor coarse jesting, which are not fitting, but rather giving of thanks."*

Isaiah 50:4; *"The Lord God has given Me The tongue of the learned, That I should know how to speak A word in season to him who is weary. He awakens Me morning by morning, He awakens My ear To hear as the learned."*

6. Have self-control

The Bible shows us that man was created by God; a tripartite being. That means He is a person made of a spirit (man is a spiritual being), a soul (man is a psychic being), and a body (man is a physical being). At the new birth (the day we accepted the salvation offered by Jesus Christ), the spirit of man is automatically and directly saved.

Soul salvation does not happen right away, but it is rather progressive. It is a process. The soul is being saved by the knowledge we have of the Word. It is therefore our responsibility to devote ourselves to the meditation of the Word of God and to prayer in order to make our soul grow. It is necessary to continually educate ourselves in the different areas of our lives (intellectual, emotional, sentimental, spiritual, etc.). As for the body, it is the responsibility of man to maintain it in the state of a perpetual servant of the Spirit of God.

It is at the new birth that we receive the Holy Spirit. But even when we receive it, our fleshly nature does not go away. The

Spirit of God only gives us the strength to tame the flesh. The Christian will therefore always be confronted with an internal battle between his carnal desires and the will of the Spirit, hence, the importance of developing self-control.

1Corinthians 9:23-27 23 *"Now this I do for the gospel's sake, that I may be partaker of it with you. 24 Do you not know that those who run in a race all run, but one receives the prize? Run in such a way that you may obtain it. 25 And everyone who competes for the prize is temperate in all things. Now they do it to obtain a perishable crown, but we for an imperishable crown. 26 Therefore I run thus: not with uncertainty. Thus I fight: not as one who beats the air. 27 But I discipline my body and bring it into subjection, lest, when I have preached to others, I myself should become disqualified."*

1Corinthians 11:27 *" In weariness and toil, in sleeplessness often, in hunger and thirst, in fastings often, in cold and nakedness."*

1 Corinthians 4:11-13 *"To the present hour we both hunger and thirst, and we are poorly clothed, and beaten, and homeless. 12 And we labor, working with our own hands. Being reviled, we bless; being persecuted, we endure; 13 being defamed, we entreat. We have been made as the filth of the world, the offscouring of all things until now."*

Romans 8:11 *"But if the Spirit of Him who raised Jesus from the dead dwells in you, He who raised Christ from the dead will also give life to your mortal bodies through His Spirit who dwells in you."*

7. Be aware of the realities of service

A good servant must be armed with the thought of suffering, meaning that he must be aware of the reality of service. Following

Jesus is a commitment that involves our entire being, spirit, soul, and body. When we decide to follow Christ, we have to give up certain things. We have to renounce fleshly desire, sin, and certain habits that lead to sin. Without renunciation, the Christianity we profess is vain! Conflicts may naturally occur in our church, in our relationships, in our home, in our family, etc., but a Christian must be able to face these difficulties and deal with them.

People living according to this world will not often agree with your decision to follow Jesus. Having noticed that they can no longer sin with you, some people might even cast you aside. For those people, it is foolishness to serve God, to give Him your time, your money, your youth, to live in chastity, and so on. You need to be aware that some people might even start persecuting you. The Lord Jesus warned us that we will be persecuted for His name's sake. He encourages us to persevere, knowing that a crown of glory is waiting for us.

Matthew 5:10-12 " *Blessed are those who are persecuted for righteousness sake, For theirs is the kingdom of heaven. 11 Blessed are you when they revile and persecute you, and say all kinds of evil against you falsely for My sake. 12 Rejoice and be exceedingly glad, for great is your reward in heaven, for so they persecuted the prophets who were before you.*"

Following Jesus implies accepting that there will be tough moments. Everything will not always be easy or rosy for you.

Matthew 16:24-25 "*Then Jesus said to His disciples, "If anyone desires to come after Me, let him deny himself, and take up his cross, and follow Me. 25 For whoever desires to save his life will lose it, but whoever loses his life for My sake will find it." If we are not ready to accept all these things, we are not yet ready to work for God."*

There is some suffering that the Master imposes on us. There is also some suffering that we impose on ourselves for the Master. To illustrate this, let us take the example of Moses who refused the privilege of being called the son of Pharaoh's daughter in order to serve his Hebrew brothers who were slaves in Egypt at that time. It was God's will that he go to them. As for Joseph, he refused to sleep with the wife of his master, Potiphar, in order to honor God. He was then falsely accused of rape and unjustly imprisoned. Yet, another example is that of Nehemiah, who refused the coveted position of king's cupbearer in order to go and help rebuild Jerusalem's wall.

1 Peter 4:1 *"Therefore, since Christ suffered for us in the flesh, arm yourselves also with the same mind, for he who has suffered in the flesh has ceased from sin. »*

Revelation 2:10 *« Do not fear any of those things which you are about to suffer. Indeed, the devil is about to throw some of you into prison, that you may be tested, and you will have tribulation ten days. Be faithful until death, and I will give you the crown of life. »*

Matthew 10:22 *« And you will be hated by all for My name's sake.*

But he who endures to the end will be saved."

8. Loyal with money

Our attitude toward money reveals the state of our hearts. Giving is an extension of our inner self. A servant needs to overcome the god "Mammon," which is the excessive love of money and wealth. Mammon is the personification of money. He becomes an idol in the heart of man, more important than God, more important than human beings. This mind-set actually dominates the world. We need to cut ourselves o from this way of operating in order to become partners with God. Our money should be used to advance the Kingdom of God.

Solomon, the wise man, gave much thought to the issue of money. According to his study, money solves many problems, but not all. It cannot solve the problem of man's inner being, which is vanity.

A servant of God who has not yet overcome greed and avarice, will never be efficient in his work and therefore will not be a good servant.

N.B.: *Let us not seek the possessions of those who come to confide in us, but rather, seek their edification.*

Matthew 6:24 *"No one can serve two masters; for either he will hate the one and love the other, or else he will be loyal to the one and despise the other. You cannot serve God and mammon."*

The Bible says that the love of money is the root of all evil. It has plunged people into many excesses. That was the case with Balaam, Korah, and many others.

2 Peter 2:15 *"They have forsaken the right way and gone astray, following the way of Balaam the son of Beor, who loved the wages of unrighteousness."*

Jude 11 *"Woe to them! For they have gone in the way of Cain, have run greedily in the error of Balaam for profit, and perished in the rebellion of Korah."*

To illustrate this, we also suggest you read the following verses: 1 Timothy 6:3-10 ; 2 Corinthians 8:1-24 ; Numbers 22:1-21.

9. A defender of the truth

A good servant must not compromise with the Word of God. Unfortunately, modern Christianity increasingly wants to please men and is approaching humanism more. God is no longer at the center of concerns. Man and his fulfillment are put above all other values, even above God. Man is thus deployed.

We see in our Christian environment a lot of complacency with the values of the present century. We have become tolerant of sin, and repentance no longer seems necessary. The Gospel is thus compromised and preaching tends to become flattering and manipulative. We are gradually moving away from the Word of God in order to become part of the world. So, we, more than ever, need servants who will speak the truth of God without compromise, but with love. Truth without love, just as love without truth does not represent God.

Jesus, the perfect model, always spoke the truth with love, except towards the Pharisees. He was harder on them because they were supposed to be role models. But, towards the people, Christ was rather gentle.

John 8:44 *"You are of your father the devil, and the desires of your father you want to do. He was a murderer from the beginning, and does not stand in the truth, because there is no truth in him. When* *he speaks a lie, he speaks from his own resources, for he is a liar and the father of it."*

2 Timothy 4:1-3 *"I charge you therefore before God and the Lord Jesus Christ, who will judge the living and the dead at His appearing and His kingdom: 2 Preach the word! Be ready in season and out of season. Convince, rebuke, exhort, with all longsuffering and teaching. 3 For the time will come when they will not endure sound doctrine, but according to their own desires, because they have itching ears, they will heap up for themselves teachers."*

N.B.: A servant appointed by God will speak of God, a servant appointed by men will speak of men, and a self-appointed servant will speak of himself.

Let us close this chapter with a reflection on how we serve: In God's eyes, what kind of servant am I?

CHAPTER 3
THE IMPORTANCE OF THE LOCAL CHURCH

3

THE IMPORTANCE OF THE LOCAL CHURCH

I. THE LOCAL CHURCH, THE ORGANIZATION OF GOD'S SERVICE ON EARTH

1. Service versus activism

In Matthew 28:19 the Lord Jesus only gives one mission to His disciples: to go and make disciples of all nations. The Lord thus entrusts this responsibility to His Church.

It is God's will that every Christian should not be limited to the simple fact of being a Christian, that is to say, to have only experienced the new birth, or even to have just attended an assembly. The Lord's will is for each of us to become disciples who later will be able to make other disciples. The Lord calls us to serve Him. We are saved to serve.

We do not serve God anyhow! We do not serve God as we want or as men want. We serve the Lord according to His Word, in other words, according to His will. The trap of men in their good works is activism. This is multiplying activities for God, not according to His will, but according to one's own pleasure or according to the human conception of things.

Revelation 3:1 ... *"I know your works, that you have a name that you are alive, but you are dead."*

The purpose of this chapter is to make us understand that in our walk with the Lord, we need to break free from activism and render acceptable service to God; the service that He asks us to do. The Lord considers service as worship and as praise. Power is released through true service.

Good intentions according to one's own convictions are not enough to serve God. One serves the Lord according to His Word. Let's take the story of David and his friend, Uzzah, as an example. They had good personal intentions concerning the return of the ark of God to Jerusalem. They wanted the worship of Yahweh to be re-established in Israel. They placed the ark of God on a new chariot driven by oxen in order to bring it back. However, they had forgotten how worship to God was to be rendered! The ark was not supposed to be placed on a beautiful new chariot driven by beautiful robust oxen, but on the shoulders of the Levites! As a result, when the ark leaned to fall, Uzzah touched it in an attempt to prevent it from falling over. The Bible says that Uzzah was struck by God and he died on the spot for having dared to touch the ark!

2 Samuel 6:6 *"And when they came to Nachon's threshing floor, Uzzah put out his hand to the ark of God and took hold of it, for the oxen stumbled. 7 Then the anger of the Lord was aroused against*

Uzzah, and God struck him there for his error; and he died there by the ark of God."

Beloved, let us be careful and take God seriously. The Bible recommends us to seek the Lord. We do not serve God just anyhow, in a disorganized manner. There is a proper way to serve Him. Let us seek His will in the Bible and submit to his Word.

Why did God establish the local churches as places of worship?

Among the principles of service to God, the Lord expects every Christian to serve in the local church. In other words, every Christian must have a fixed local church, and every Christian must have a fixed Pastor!

Hebrews 10:25 " *not forsaking the assembling of ourselves together, as is the manner of some, but exhorting one another, and so much the more as you see the Day approaching."*

The apostles were themselves members of local churches:

Acts 13:1 *"Now in the church that was at Antioch there were certain prophets and teachers: Barnabas, Simeon who was called Niger, Lucius of Cyrene, Manaen who had been brought up with Herod the tetrarch, and Saul."*

1 Peter 4:10 *"As each one has received a gift, minister it to one another, as good stewards of the manifold grace of God."*

Acts 2:41 *"Then those who gladly received his word were baptized; and that day about three thousand souls were added to them. 42 And* *they continued steadfastly in the apostles' doctrine and fellowship, in the breaking of bread, and in prayers."*

The passage, in **Acts 2:41** shows that the first Christians persevered in the 4 pillars of faith which are: the teaching of the Apostles, fellowship, prayers, and the breaking of bread.

In order to grow spiritually, the believer must apply these fundamental principles, and they can only be applied in the context of a local church. It is impossible otherwise. One cannot be a disciple of Jesus without being attached to a fixed local church and without putting the gift one has received to the service of others.

Discipleship always involves a stable relationship with one's instructors.

2. The difference between the universal and the local church

We have seen that the Lord saved us to be His disciples. Being a disciple of Christ is to be attached to His Word and to His Person; to Who He is.

Since God is Spirit and thus invisible and cannot be perceived by man, we cannot limit discipleship to the dimension of mere personal faith. God is invisible and always works on earth through men. Man consequently occupies an important place for God and for humans among themselves. It is, therefore, necessary to consider the practical aspect of discipleship as well. The Bible shows us that each Christian is a member of the body of Christ and that together we all form the Church. Hence, the importance of considering its nature and its structure, because it is the place par excellence for the manifestation of the will and the work of the Lord.

It is the Lord Jesus Himself who established the Church by the Holy Spirit at Pentecost and who is the Head. In the Bible, the Church is compared to the Body of Christ.

Ephesians 5:23 *"For the husband is head of the wife, as also Christ is head of the church; and He is the Savior of the body."*

1 Corinthians 12:27-28 *"Now you are the body of Christ, and members individually. 28 And God has appointed these in the church: first apostles, second prophets, third teachers, after that miracles, then gifts of healings, helps, administrations, varieties of tongues."*

In order to understand the functioning of the Church, it is necessary to understand its two dimensions, the visible and the invisible. We must be able to distinguish between the universal Church and the local Church.

When a person receives Jesus as Lord and Savior with his whole heart, he becomes a child of God. He is then part of the body of Christ and has a particular and unique gift. The Universal Church is made up of all true believers. The Universal Church is called the invisible Church because only God knows the hearts, knows who is really saved and who is subject to Him and who is not. Faith is individual, not hereditary. The invisible Church, therefore, has no fixed location.

But the Lord designed the Church to be visible on earth, to serve as a witness, and to worship Him! Given that we, as humans, are not formed of spirit alone, but have a body and are part of the visible world, this is where the importance of a local assembly comes in. The materialization of the invisible Church takes place at the level of the local church. The local church is the visible church and can be defined as a concrete Christian community led by a Pastor.

Matthew 16:18 *"is a verse that shows us the universal dimension of the church established by Christ, "And I also say to you that you are Peter, and on this rock, I will build My church, and the gates of*

Hades shall not prevail against it."

Matthew 18:17 shows us the local dimension of the Church for the exercise of its management, its doctrine, and its internal discipline, *"And if he refuses to hear them, tell it to the church. But if he refuses even to hear the church, let him be to you like a heathen and a tax collector."*

In chapter 2 of the book of Acts, we see these two dimensions of the Church. The Holy Spirit came down on all those who were present in the upper room that day. As a result of the preaching and testimonies of the disciples that were gathered together, several thousands of other people, including foreigners who did not live in Jerusalem, were converted to the Lord Jesus Christ. All of these people are part of the universal Church. This upper room was the first local church in Jerusalem, which made it possible for several thousands of people to become part of the universal Church.

In Greek, the word church is "ekklesia," which means the assembly of those who have responded to the call of God. When we come together like this, we form the bride of Christ. We are His body on earth. Each member of the body is important. The Lord calls His people to gather, unite, and be seen in a specific place. The Lord calls each Christian to be located in a specific place, to belong to a local assembly, and thus to bear visible witness to his personal faith.

3. The organization of the churches

Any gathering requires leadership and structure, to ensure the best functioning and productivity. The service of each member is beneficial and must be coordinated for an effective result. God, being a good manager, has appointed pastors to ensure the functioning of local gathering.

Pastors have a great responsibility to the people of God. In **Ephesians 4:11**, the Bible shows us how Christ, the Head of the Church, o ers the ve-fold ministry of apostle, evangelist, prophet, pastor, and teacher as a gift, in order to edify His body. The 5 ministries consist of the work of the leadership of each local church in particular!

Ephesians 4:7-16 *"But to each one of us, grace was given according to the measure of Christ's gift. 8 Therefore He says "When He ascended on high, He led captivity captive, And gave gifts to men." 9 (Now this, "He ascended"—what does it mean but that He also first descended into the lower parts of the earth? 10 He who descended is also the One who ascended far above all the heavens, that He might fill all things.)*

11 And He Himself gave some to be apostles, some prophets, some evangelists, and some pastors and teachers, 12 for the equipping of the saints for the work of ministry, for the edifying of the body of Christ, 13 till we all come to the unity of the faith and of the knowledge of the Son of God, to a perfect man, to the measure of the stature of the fullness of Christ; 14 that we should no longer be children, tossed to and fro and carried about with every wind of doctrine, by the trickery of men, in the cunning craftiness of deceitful plotting, 15 but, speaking the truth in love, may grow up in all things into Him who is the head—Christ—16 from whom the whole body, joined and knit together by what every joint supplies, according to the effective working by which every part does its share, causes growth of the body for the edifying of itself in love."

It is interesting to point out that it is Christ, the second person of the trinity, the head of the Church, who gives gifts to men- those who are called to assure the visible leadership of the local churches on earth for His Church. Christ only gives the ministry gifts. The Bible shows that each person of the trinity gives distinct gifts.

There are gifts given by God the Father (natural talents), gifts that are given by the Holy Spirit (gifts of the Spirit, supernatural equipment), and those given by Christ, the Good Shepherd, such as to church leaders (gifts of ministry); given to those who are the shepherds of the local churches.

As stated in Ephesians 4, Christ has appointed shepherds, to perfect, unite and coordinate the service of God's people (the saints). The local church is the place chosen by Christ to guarantee the care, nurture, guidance, and follow-up of His disciples, furthermore, a well-organized and effective service of the people of God.

Alfred Kuen[6] said that there is nothing more beautiful, nor more effective, than life in a local church.

---

[6] *A. Kuen.Encyclopedia of Questions, Ed. Emmaus, Saint-Légier Switzerland 2012 -p.379*

II. THE LOCAL CHURCH, THE SPIRITUAL FAMILY

1. *The God of families*

We know that we have to take care of our bodies, our intimate and professional relationships, our families, our studies, our careers, etc. But, what about the spiritual part of us? We usually overlook it. And yet, our blessing depends on it.

Even though we are called to work in the secular field, being Christians, it is necessary to remember that our lives are structured around the spiritual.

The Bible teaches us that the human being is a tripartite being. God created us body, soul, and spirit. We are therefore physical, psychic, and spiritual beings. We need to take care of each part of our being.

We are all born into a family one day and are expected to grow; to flourish in all areas of our lives. Man always needs to belong to a family in order to grow properly. To be deprived of a family creates enormous wounds and unfulfilled emotional needs. These wounds need to be healed in order for a man to be able to start a healthy family of his own. The family is therefore very important.

*For more information on this subject, see our "Fruit of the Spirit" module.

From a physical point of view, the Lord gives a biological family to man. From a spiritual point of view, the Lord, who is a responsible Father, gives to the born-again man (a person that has accepted Jesus Christ as his Lord and Savior), a visible spiritual family, which is the local church. Within, God gives him a Pastor, brothers, and sisters. This structure is ideal for man's growth, protection, and development. The Christian takes his first steps in the faith. People discover their true identity within the local church. It is there that one benefits and applies one's rights and duties.

For those without a biological family, the local church can provide comfort and make up for the lack of love and guidance. God has always worked with families in His methodology. Take the example of Moses. When He appears to him in the burning bush, He reminds him that He is the God of his fathers: He tells him that He is the God of Abraham, Isaac and Jacob. In the Bible, the Lord presents Himself as God of the fathers. In Malachi 4:6, He says that "he will turn the hearts of the fathers to the children, And the hearts of the children to their fathers, Lest I come and strike the earth with a curse." This verse depicts the concept of the restoration of families.

In the Old Testament, we can see that the Passover lamb was always to be eaten as a family. The 12 spies sent to Canaan were chosen according to the 12 tribes of Israel, each of the 12 spies thus represented each family of Israel. The church is nothing more than the culmination of this notion of families.

We serve a God who takes "the family" very seriously. We do not serve God in a haphazard and messy way. God is a God of order. He is the God of families, as seen in **Ephesians 3:15** *"from whom the whole family in heaven and earth is named."*

The whole of nature teaches us this principle. Consider the plants, the animals, the spiritual world, the political world, the tribes, the nations, etcetera. Everything that was born, has been spawned from someone else. Only God exists by Himself. No one comes into the world by himself. You become a Christian because someone teaches you about salvation. We do not grow in faith alone, but because the Pastor explains the Bible to us and makes it real in us.

2. The Fraternal Fellowship

Having a fixed local church is therefore essential for a Christian. The Christian life is not a life of isolation. It is a life in a community. The Lord asks us to gather together to worship and serve Him together. We are not independent in the body of Christ. We work together in solidarity. Each of us is a member of the body and acts in his or her domain, relating to the talents and gifts we have received.

Acts 2:46-47 *"So continuing daily with one accord in the temple, and breaking bread from house to house, they ate their food with gladness and simplicity of heart, 47 praising God and having favor with all the people. And the Lord added to the church daily those who were being saved."*

Without the community, our Christianity is severely restricted. We are called to give and to receive from others. We are called to make our invisible faith visible, and to openly testify what God is doing in us. Since God cannot be seen, when He is served, it is men who pro t from it. It is fellowship; the attachment to a fixed local church that allows the practice of all the teachings received from the Bible, such as the practice of love, the edification, and exhortation that the Holy Spirit has personally inspired, the teachings, the evangelization, the exercise of gifts and talents, the transfer of anointing, and so on. Know that the anointing is never given only for oneself, but is meant to be transmitted to others as well. The Gospel is a blessing to us and must also be given to others. Having brothers and sisters in the faith edifies us and strengthens our prayer life. Christians of the same community form a body together and need each other to progress. So they form a visible family.

Since God does not accept disorder, it is, therefore, IMPERATIVE to understand how a family functions.

3. Beware of isolation and independence

To say that I do not need a local church assembly because I have a Bible and I belong to the Universal Church, is reasoning contrary to the Word of God. The Bible shows us that when we are saved, we belong to a new family, that is, to a new society with new standards. The Word of God asks us not to abandon our local assembly.

A servant who does not have a fixed local church is a man who is not subject to authority, to the supervision of a Pastor. He is a Christian without any spiritual reference point. The service of such a person to God lacks coordination, perfection, and unity intended and established by the Lord. There will therefore be no efficiency or power in his actions. To illustrate this, let us take the example of evangelism.

How can we evangelize without being attached to a local church? The newly converted person needs to be oriented in discipleship. To which church should you direct them if you do not even have one yourself? The person newly converted to Christ needs a concrete and visible example. They need to experience concrete and real communion and love. Bringing a soul to Jesus is an important task and a good thing. A soul once won must be guided in order to grow spiritually. The mentoring of a soul also requires a lot of work. The novice Christian needs to be introduced to his new family and bene t from the affection of the brothers in Christ. He needs to be blessed by the anointing of the choir members, the intercessors, and other brothers and sisters in the faith. He thus learns to praise, pray, to worship God, and to exercise love, thanks to the community.

He needs to be strengthened by his Pastor. If a person lacks guidance, the risk of returning to the world is great. And it will be even more di cult to bring that soul back to the Lord. Therefore, evangelistic service cannot be done in isolation. Each of us is a part, a member of a body. We cannot relocate a member.

This is why the mission entrusted to us by the Lord consists of making disciples and not limiting ourselves to solely evangelize. The same is true for any other service rendered unto God. Without attachment to a church and without supervision from the shepherd, the service is of little, if any, value.

If one wants to preach, it is necessary to go to an existing local church. We cannot preach to the universal Church. We need to go to an existing structure, to a concrete assembly. This shows that local churches are important. If there are no more local churches, we will no longer be able to preach, exhort, exercise our gifts, sing, testify, etc.! Any given preaching requires being put into practice. The Christian will be able to practice it within his community. But, if he does not have one, how will this be possible?

Without a fixed church, a Christian loses a lot. This lack has a negative impact on his spiritual growth. At a wedding, we seek the pastoral blessing. It is, of course, the Pastor of your local congregation who will bless your marriage. When the time has come to get married, it is not normal for a Christian to have to look for a Pastor who will bless his marriage, at the last moment. A Christian is supposed to belong to a fixed community. If the Christian does not have a church because he believes he belongs to the universal Church, he will have to ask the Pastor of the universal Church to come and bless his marriage, which is not possible.

The same is applicable after a loss. It is natural that members of the community will be able to support the bereaved person. His or her Pastor will lead the ceremony. But how can this be done if one does not have a fixed assembly? Why look for a pastor whom you do not even know, to whom you have no spiritual attachment, to come and bless your wedding or to conduct a funeral ceremony? If one considers that as a Christian, the care and supervision of a pastor is not important, why should it be so on an ad-hoc basis for a particular event?

Our prayer is that the Lord deliver us from blindness and activism, so that we may understand the concept of service. God told Moses to tell Pharaoh "Let my people go, so that they may serve me (to worship me)." Let this be your portion in the name of Jesus.

The Bible shows us that the first disciples were identified as Christians while they were involved in their local church which was located in Antioch.

Acts 11:26 *"And when he had found him, he brought him to Antioch. So it was that for a whole year they assembled with the church and taught a great many people. And the disciples were first called Christians in Antioch."*

Throughout the Bible, God's servants who excelled in their service, such as the apostle Paul, respected this principle of belonging to a local church.

4. The trap of the virtual world

Today, new technologies allow us to follow worship services, and teachings and even allow us to communicate remotely, all while staying at home.

While it is true that digital tools have brought several advantages, it must be understood that online broadcasting will never replace real and concrete fraternal communion. The Church will never be virtual because it operates as a family. We cannot replace our local church with the internet. That is laziness. A close relationship with a shepherd and between brothers and sisters in the faith is necessary to ensure one's Christian growth. The internet is only useful to the extent that it helps, complements, and reinforces belonging to a community that must be and remains real.

5. The work of the enemy

We cannot ignore the fact that certain factors have tarnished the image of the family, in the minds of many people. Unfortunately, many people do not have good family experiences. In Belgium[7], for example, one in three teenagers has divorced parents. Several parents have been absent, failing in their responsibilities. Some even went so far as abusing their own o spring. There are thus, no clear references points.

Cults also play a negative role in the concept of the family. Through their abuse, they leave scars and traumas that are di cult to repair. Living with such bad realities, it becomes problematic for some people to trust an institution like a church.

May the Lord help us and give us the strength to be understanding and patient towards our brothers and sisters in the faith. Let us show God's love to the discouraged. God is able to heal inner wounds and x broken references.

Our prayer is that the Lord will heal our churches and that we may experience the benefits of unity and brotherly love which is absolutely necessary for the development of every human being.

Despite the ravages of evil, we must not lose sight of the purpose of God's creation. God did not create man to live alone. Humans are social beings. The trees that grow in the forest are straight and long because they grow together. The isolated tree, on the other hand, fails to reach its maximum growth and is twisted.

The church is a family. In order to understand it, we have to get out of the materialistic and hedonistic logic of life. The family does not function like a market or a supermarket. You

---

[7] *Articles published on november 25, 2019 by RTL (www.rtl.be) « Belgium is one of the Europe's Countries where the divorce rate is the highest; one teenager in 3 has divorced parents."*

cannot buy or sell a family. You cannot abandon your family. The family is governed by the authority of the parents, with love and self-sacrifice.

The notions of "servant" and "service" to God are opposed to the individualistic notions of the sole pursuit of chasing happiness, pleasure, consumerism, etc., that are overvalued in our present-day societies. Rather, the concept of "service" implies the concepts of commitment and attachment.

6. Some thoughts of reflection

To conclude this point, we offer you a time of refection and meditation regarding our responsibility towards our local church, which is the work of Christ on earth. Let us take the time to meditate and pray on this subject. Many blessings come from serving God according to His will.

The Bible tells us in **Exodus 23:25** *"So you shall serve the Lord your God, and He will bless your bread and your water. And I will take sickness away from the midst of you."*

- — Do we have a fixed local church? Do we have a fixed Pastor?
- — What are we doing to sustain the life of our local church?
- — Do we take care of our spiritual family in terms of commitment of time and material resources?
- — Can unbelievers identify us as Christians by our testimony of commitment, unity, and love?

- Have we fallen into the traps of desire for
  independence - the superficial and unsustainable
  lifestyle that characterize our societies today?
- Do we consider the church as a market where we come
  to consume or sell in case of need, even if it means
  eventually paying or being paid for a service, and then
  leaving?
- Do we consider the church as a fair where everyone does
  as they wish, thus rejecting the established authorities?
- Do we see brothers and sisters in faith as blessings at all
  times or do we only find them interesting when they
  help us achieve our goals?
- Are we ready to love our neighbor, to serve him so that
  he fully realizes the purpose of his existence as intended
  by God, and do this without expecting anything in
  return?

Just as Nehemiah did during his time, we want to rebuild the
walls of the local church. Let us get up together and build!

III. THE ROLE OF THE PASTOR

1. The Pastoral role mandated by Christ Himself

The local church can therefore be defined as the family God
intended to ensure the growth of His disciples. We can also
compare it to a sheepfold, and the Lord Jesus Christ as its Good
Shepherd.

Ephesians 4:11 shows us that it is Christ, the head of the
Church, the Good Shepherd, who Himself commissions
human shepherds to lead the local churches. Chapters 2 and 3

of the book of Revelation show us that the Lord addresses each angel in charge of each church to deliver a message concerning the faithful members of that assembly. These angels are none other than the Pastors of each of these churches:

"Write to the angel of the church of Ephesus, … of Smyrna, … of Pergamum, … of Thyatira, … of Sardis, … of Philadelphia, … of Laodicea, …"

The epistles were also addressed to the churches through the leaders of the local assemblies.

So, there are many churches and many pastors. These shepherds are listed in the heavenly book. They were commissioned by Christ Himself. The Bible strictly forbids self-proclaimed pastors; it is Christ who gives this call! **Hebrews 5:4** states that *"And no man takes this honor to himself, but he who is called by God, just as Aaron was."*

There is always a way to enter a function. Take the example of doctors. To become a doctor, it is the medical degree obtained that gives access to the practice of the profession. The same is true for pharmacists. If you open a pharmacy or practice as a doctor without a degree, or without having been mandated, you are engaging in banditry. And, the patients of this type of fraudulent service put their lives in danger!

Each profession has its own way of authorizing the exercise of its function. The same is true for the pastoral function. One becomes a Pastor by divine call.

John 15:16 "You did not choose Me, but I chose you and appointed you that you should go and bear fruit, and that your fruit should remain, that whatever you ask the Father in My name He may give you."

Acts 1:24 "And they prayed and said, "You, O Lord, who know the hearts of all, show which of these two You have chosen."

We want to warn about the motivations that drive some people to become pastors or to do pastoral work by gathering people around them. Know, that one:

- does not become a pastor by obtaining a degree in theology,
- does not become a pastor because they wish to become one,
- does not become a pastor because there is no church in the area where you live,
- does not become a pastor because a group of people want them to become a pastor,
- does not become a pastor because one does not appreciate the work done by another pastor,
- does not become a pastor on the basis of his natural leadership skills,
- does not become a pastor out of rebellion.

You only become one, when Christ mandates you!

In other words, you do not start a local church because you have obtained a degree in theology, or because you want to, or because a group of people want you to start the work, or because a church does not function well in your opinion, or because there is no church in the area where you live, or because you have a natural ability to gather people around you, or as a result of a rebellion. A local church only opens on the basis of a mandate delegated by the Lord Jesus Christ Himself!

God gives the "angel" of the local church a vision, a particular message for the need of the sheep that the Lord has entrusted to him. The Lord then gives the message to the messenger and the team.

2. Only one direction

In a family, there is only one father, not two.

In a church, there is only one Pastor. There is only one vision, not two. A body has only one head and moves in the same direction. It is impossible for a body to go in two directions at once. A body with two heads is not a body. It is impossible for a church to achieve its mission if it does not recognize the authority and importance of its Pastor over it. It is also impossible for the shepherd to achieve the goals of the church alone. He absolutely needs the other members of the body of Christ to do so.

Depending on the need and the size of a church, the Pastor delegates elders, deacons and preachers to extend the vision. These things are done in order, as it was the case with Timothy, Joshua, Samuel and the other biblical figures.

Numbers 27:18-20 "And the Lord said to Moses: "Take Joshua the son of Nun with you, a man in whom is the Spirit, and lay your hand on him; 19 set him before Eleazar the priest and before all the congregation, and inaugurate him in their sight. 20 And you shall give some of your authority to him, that all the congregation of the children of Israel may be obedient."

3. Church Model left by Christ?

The Lord Jesus Christ did not leave a clear model of church organization. The basic structure of each assembly is the presence of a Pastor-leader.

During His lifetime, Christ did not found a local church. He entrusted this mission to the apostles who were sufficiently equipped to carry out this task. It is through them and through their sons in the faith, the apostolic fathers, that we can be inspired by the model of the first generation church.

The apostles have laid a solid evangelical foundation that will never change. The apostolic fathers also developed a set of traditions that addressed the practical concerns of early Christians regarding worship, preaching, teaching and the mission. Just as the first Christians did, each congregation builds its work on the evangelical foundation laid by the apostles. The diversity of each community is made by the way in which we build on this foundation.

Ephesians 2:20-21 *"having been built on the foundation of the apostles and prophets, Jesus Christ Himself being the chief cornerstone, 21 in whom the whole building, being fitted together, grows into a holy temple in the Lord,"*

1 Corinthians 3:10 *"According to the grace of God which was given to me, as a wise master builder I have laid the foundation, and another builds on it. But let each one take heed how he builds on it."*

The mission of the Church, which manifests itself in evangelization, edification and worship, therefore remains universal. The organization of each assembly is different since it depends on the divine mandate, the place and the need for an assembly. It is therefore useless to try to copy the model of another church.

The Pygmies' realities, for instance, are different from those experienced by Westerners. Their working methods will therefore, be different. This is what makes each minister or head-pastor, when he receives the mandate to build, to possess particular traits that are different from other shepherds.

Since every human being is unique, we will always be confronted with diversity. Even if all had the same Lord and the same objectives, the church of Sardis was still not the same as the one of Philadelphia. The apostle Paul did not work in the same way as Apostle Peter. For the same Gospel message, the Bible presents us with 4 different approaches: Matthew, Mark, Luke and John. We find common features in these 4 books, but also, mostly different perceptions. It all depends on the personality of each one, or on the audience of each one.

Titus 1:5-6 *"For this reason I left you in Crete, that you should set in order the things that are lacking, and appoint elders in every city as I commanded you— 6 if a man is blameless, the husband of one wife, having faithful children not accused of dissipation or insubordination."*

1 Timothy 1:3 *"As I urged you when I went into*

Macedonia—remain in Ephesus that you may charge some that they teach no other doctrine."

These verses show the apostle Paul establishing leaders in different communities: Titus in Crete, Timothy in Ephesus. He entrusts them with particular missions depending on the realities of each community, but whose goal is to reach the same objective, such as unity in the independence of the churches.

Ephesians 4:4-6 *"There is one body and one Spirit, just as you were called in one hope of your calling; 5 one Lord, one faith, one baptism; 6 one God and Father of all, who is above all, and through all, and in you all.7 But to each one of us grace was given according to the measure of Christ's gift …"*

The stars are all different. They do not shine evenly bright and they do not have the same purposes. But, each of them serve to the doxology, to the glory of God in a different way.

There are different ways of organizing the functioning of each community. But, all are led by a shepherd-in-charge, work as a family and are based on the evangelical foundation of the apostles.

4. The Church's Mission

The church has only received one mission. The evangelical world calls it The Great Mission or The Great Commission. It was issued by Christ in **Matthew 28:19**, and consists of "Go therefore and make disciples of all the nations, baptizing them in the name of the Father and of the Son and of the Holy Spirit."

This mission is therefore unique, and its execution involves 3 dimensions:

- the first is horizontal. This is evangelization. The dimension is said to be horizontal because the relationship is directed towards the (fellow) man;
- the second dimension is edification. It is circular because the Christian needs to be regularly edified and also needs to edify others;
- the third dimension is vertical. It is about the worship and service that the Christian offers to God.

In order to train a disciple, we must first evangelize to bring the soul to Christ. The goal is for the soul to become a worshiper of the Lord, to serve God. To become a worshiper, the soul needs to regularly be edified, taught and commune with his brothers in the faith.

5. The duties of a Pastor

It is necessary to clarify the role of the Pastor, so that we can better understand what we should expect of him.

The authority of the Pastor is limited to the level of the management of his local church and nowhere else. The Pastor does not have to do everything. He does not have all the gifts that exist on earth. But, he is called to perform a particular task which characterizes him as a pastor. These duties are mentioned in Ephesians 4.

Ephesians 4:7-16 *"But to each one of us grace was given according to the measure of Christ's gift. 8 Therefore He says:*

"When He ascended on high, He led captivity captive, And gave gifts to men." 9 (Now this, "He ascended"—what does it mean but that

He also first descended into the lower parts of the earth? 10 He who descended is also the One who ascended far above all the heavens, that He might fill all things.)

11 And He Himself gave some to be apostles, some prophets, some evangelists, and some pastors and teachers, 12 for the equipping of the saints for the work of ministry, for the edifying of the body of Christ, 13 till we all come to the unity of the faith and of the knowledge of the Son of God, to a perfect man, to the measure of the stature of the fullness of Christ; 14 that we should no longer be children, tossed to and fro and carried about with every wind of doctrine, by the trickery of men, in the cunning craftiness of deceitful plotting, 15 but, speaking the truth in love, may grow up in all things into Him who is the head—Christ— 16 from whom the whole body, joined and knit together by what every joint supplies, according to the effective working by which every part does its share, causes growth of the body for the edifying of itself in love."

The Lord Jesus therefore established pastors in order to:

5.1. "Perfect the saints"

The Greek word "perfect," means to prepare, to equip, to instruct, to correct, to complete. The Pastor is therefore above all, a preacher. But, beware, he is not only a preacher. He must also be a teacher of the Word of God. Preaching consists in announcing, presenting the Gospel. Teaching is not the announcement, but the explanation of the Gospel. Its aim is to train disciples.

The Pastor is an anointed man filled with the Word of God, able to preach and train disciples.

5.2. "For the work of the ministry and the edification of the body of Christ"

The Pastor helps identify a disciple's gift in order to make it available to the church. His job is to equip each one in his ministry. The goal is to accomplish the mission of the local church. He therefore coordinates the different gifts and helps the people of God to live in love and maturity within their fellowship in the local assembly.

5.3. "The goal is to come to the unity of the faith, to the knowledge of the son of God and to maturity"

To make the people of God understand the mission, and the vision of the church, the Pastor must teach. It is this teaching that allows the believers to develop unity to achieve the mission of the church. Unity should not be seen as uniformity. The unity we refer to includes the diversity of each of the members and the complementarity of each other in order to achieve the objectives of the church.

The Pastor works so that each member of his congregation can come to "know God." He will do his best to ensure that his parishioners understand salvation and receive Christ. He promotes a life of intimacy, prayer with the Lord, listening to the Word of God, obedience and the fear of God. He thus, leads the people of God towards maturity, that is, to aim to be like Jesus.

5.4. 'Speaking the truth in love"

The pastor also promotes good fellowship and the practice of love within the community. He himself manifests love and faithfulness to his parishioners, and promotes the development of their respective ministries.

5.5. *"In order to grow"*

The Lord, therefore, established Pastors in order to train His people towards maturity, so that His people should no longer be in a "child's state," meaning, a state of mind where one is carried away by every wind of doctrine, deceptions of men or wiles of seduction of the present age.

Colossians 2:8 *"Beware lest anyone cheat you through philosophy and empty deceit, according to the tradition of men, according to the basic principles of the world, and not according to Christ."*

5.6. *"Coordinate the members of the body in order to form a solid assembly"*

The Pastor leads the church to draw from Christ, the strength to accomplish all these objectives. He must coordinate the different gifts and talents of each member in order to carry out the mission of the church. The believers must be able to flourish in their ministry.

A pastor must be loyal and faithful to the sheep entrusted to him by the Lord. We thus, recognize a pastor by his big heart filled with love and patience, by his ability to teach, instruct, and correct, help a person grow spiritually, and by his leadership skills. The Pastor is able to equip the people of God to serve the Lord in the church. He transmits the fear of God. He awakens in hearts the desire to pray, study the Word, and practice it.

A pastor is a man who is filled with the Word of God, the fear of God, and His presence. He will not copy sermons elsewhere to transmit them. He is sufficiently prepared to know the needs of his sheep and to feed them.

IV. THE IMPORTANCE OF COLLABORATORS

A pastor cannot carry out the mission of the church alone. No leader, no matter how great his calling, can accomplish a vision on his own. He always needs collaborators.

The Bible shows us that the apostle Paul had at least 66 collaborators who took his ministry to greater heights. Collaborators are able, not only to reproduce the vision of the church, but also to expand it.

1. How to choose your collaborators?

The best collaborators are the people that the Pastor himself has mentored and seen grow. We can call them his "children in the faith." This is how the Lord Jesus Christ did it. He trained only 12 disciples and made them apostles. And they are the ones who have allowed the work of Christ to spread throughout the world.

As a pastor, you should not seek for "other people's children," that is, Christians trained by other people, to make them your collaborators! This is laziness and it is disruptive to other churches. Moreover, it is also extremely rare for a church to grow with collaborators trained by other people. These "foreign" collaborators often become a source of conflict.

If some "foreign children" come to your church to work with you, we advise you to pray for guidance from the Lord. Also, check the background of these people. It is important to know the circumstances that led them to leave their old church. If it was due to insubordination and multiple complaints, we advise you to refuse to work with such people. A rebel remains a rebel for life. He risks repeating the same conflicts and destroying your congregation.

Let us not forget that the role of a shepherd is to protect his sheepfold. Redirect him to his former church. This is what God told Hagar when she was running away from Sarai. God told her to return to her mistress (female master), Sarai, and mend fences.

Genesis 16:8-9 *"And He said, "Hagar, Sarai's maid, where have you come from, and where are you going?"*

She said, "I am fleeing from the presence of my mistress Sarai." 9 The Angel of the Lord said to her, "Return to your mistress, and submit yourself under her hand."

If you still have to work with them, we advise you to clearly de ne the framework. Your best collaborators will be your children in the faith. Let them practice, even if they make mistakes. They will improve with practice.

2. Called or appointed collaborators

Collaborators can access the status of elders in an assembly. The Senior Pastor delegates his duties to them in order to carry out the mission of the church.

We have 2 categories of elders: Those who are called "presbuteros" and those who are called "episkopos." Their role is to assist the Senior Pastor in his duties and to extend the vision of the local church. They must protect their sheepfold church, watch over the propagation of sound doctrine, fight against heresies, maintain peace among the members and participate in the achievement of the objectives of their assembly. These elders may also be called pastors.

2.1. Called collaborators

The Greek word for "called elder" in the Bible is "presbuteros[8]." This term means *bishop, presbyter, elder.* These are people who have received an authentic call from the Lord Jesus Christ in one of the 5 ministries: apostle, evangelist, prophet, pastor, and teacher.

The Apostle Peter, Barnabas, Simeon, Lucius of Cyrene, and Manahen had been referred to as "called elders" as the following biblical verses show:

1 Peter 5:1-4 *"The elders who are among you I exhort, I who am a fellow elder and a witness of the sufferings of Christ, and also a partaker of the glory that will be revealed: 2 Shepherd the flock of God which is among you, serving as overseers, not by compulsion but willingly, not for dishonest gain but eagerly; 3 nor as being lords over those entrusted to you, but being examples to the flock; 4 and when the Chief Shepherd appears, you will receive the crown of glory that does not fade away."*

Acts 13:1-3 *"Now in the church that was at Antioch there were certain prophets and teachers: Barnabas, Simeon who was called Niger, Lucius of Cyrene, Manaen who had been brought up with Herod the tetrarch,*

---

[8] « Presbuteros » *taken from the greek strongs 4245*

and Saul. 2 As they ministered to the Lord and fasted, the Holy Spirit said, "Now separate to Me Barnabas and Saul for the work to which I have called them." 3 Then, having fasted and prayed, and laid hands on them, they sent them away."

Called elders are advised to work for their church full-time. Indeed, a person who has received an authentic call in one of the 5 ministries is a gift to the church. He must give himself entirely to it, by taking the risk of depending on the Lord to provide for his needs.

2.2. Appointed collaborators

The Greek word used in the Bible for an "appointed elder" is "episkopos[9]". This term means an attendant, an overseer, a supervisor, a bishop, or a guardian.

These elders are thus appointed on the basis of the criteria established by Paul and Peter in order to ensure the functioning of their assembly. These people are usually not called into one of the 5 ministries.

It is following the delegation of the shepherd-leader that they exercise the pastoral duties. And it is within this context that the Bible advises to aspire to the o ce of bishop.

1 Timothy 3:1 *"This is a faithful saying: If a man desires the position of a bishop, he desires a good work."*

Acts 14:23 *"So when they had appointed elders in every church, and prayed with fasting, they commended them to the Lord in whom they had believed."*

---

[9] *« Episkopos » taken from the greek strongs 1985*

Titus 1:5 *"For this reason I left you in Crete, that you should set in order the things that are lacking, and appoint elders in every city as I commanded you ..."*

They are advised to continue working in the secular eld in order to support themselves.

V. DUTIES OF THE DISCIPLE

1 Peter 2:2 *"As newborn babes, desire the pure milk of the word, that you may grow thereby."*

The duty of the disciple is to seek growth, apply the principles, and protect his church. The disciple puts his abilities at the service of others and contributes by his example and testimony to the progress of the community.

In an excerpt from the document drawn up by the Association des Églises Évangéliques Baptistes de la Langue Française "Ce qu'est un bon member," it is asked that a parishioner and member reserve a fair priority of his time, his forces, and his resources to his church[10] ...

1 Peter 4:10 *"As each one has received a gift, minister it to one another, as good stewards of the manifold grace of God."*

Acts 2:41–42 *"Those who accepted his message were baptized, and about three thousand were added to their number that day. 42They devoted themselves to the apostles' teaching and to fellowship, to the breaking of bread and to prayer." NIV*

---

[10] *A. Kuen.Encyclopedia of Questions, Ed. Emmaus, Saint-Légier Switzerland 2012 -p.582*

VI. THE LIMITS OF RELATIONSHIPS IN THE LOCAL CHURCH, THE IMPORTANCE OF RESPECTING EACH OTHER'S PRIVATE LIVES

The local church is a family. This also means that our relationships within our assemblies have limits. And we must be able to set them according to our realities and needs.

We have many different aspects of our lives, and the Bible says there is a time for everything. There are therefore limits to be established in everything. We must organize our time in such a way as to find a balance, by setting clear boundaries for each of our lives: our job (or studies), our families, our relationships, our friends, our hobbies, our Christian life, the fulfillment of our civic duties, our health, etc.

1. The limits of the Pastor's authority

A pastor's authority is limited to the functioning of the local church for which he is responsible. Outside of this framework, a pastor has no authority.

The relationship he maintains with the believers is limited to the Christian life within the congregation and not beyond. A pastor is not responsible for the family lives of the members of his church. He cannot interfere in the private lives of the believers and cannot make decisions for them.

At a spiritual level, a pastor cannot force the free will that God has given to each man to want to serve Him or not. He cannot control his followers, he cannot force a person to convert and he cannot force a person to obey the Word of God. Let us keep in mind, that we are servants of God and not of men. It is only towards God that we are "doulos."

Luke 12:14 *"But He said to him, "Man, who made me a judge or an arbitrator over you?"*

Pastoral authority is limited to bringing people back to their own conscience. The Pastor can awaken the desire to pray in people's hearts, the desire to seek God. But he will never be able to pray and seek God for them. He can help the believers to discover their respective ministries. But he will never be able to discover it or exercise it for them. This is everyone's personal responsibility. Only God will judge us on the last day. We cannot judge our fellow man, or the quality of his service.

If the Pastor cannot impose obedience to God, he can even less impose his personal convictions in any other field, for example in regard to politics, clothing, health care, finances, etc. What is true for the Pastor towards his parishioners/members, goes for the believers among themselves, and also for the believers towards the Pastor. We must respect each other's privacy and free will. We are not allowed to judge others.

Fellowship is a true bliss when done with love, respect, and freedom. Respecting people's private lives brings many blessings to an assembly.

2. Sectarian Excesses

When the boundaries of privacy are broken, the church becomes a cult and the Pastor, a manipulator. So let us be very careful! We must look after the well-being of the sheepfold and correct this type of defect as soon as possible, when it arises.

According to the Bible, regarding the order of priorities, the church is not the rst priority for a Christian! In the eyes of God, the worker is more important than the work:

- The number one priority for a Christian is God. It is about his personal communion with the Lord;
- In the 2nd position, we have the marital home, the children;
- In the 3rd position, we have work;
- The church only comes after these 3 essential things. So let's organize our time properly according to our means and priorities.

Some Christians have developed bad habits. Some people go to church every day while they still have to manage their homes and children! They attend all the social activities organized in the church and are thus, busy every weekend. When do these people find time for their own personal meditations with the Lord? Consequently, their homes are left neglected and they do not give enough time to their children, partners, friends, and families! Professional activities and projects are neglected. However, the Bible declares that he who does not work will not eat either! If not having time to give to God's work is a bad thing, neglecting priorities is another.

Beloved, time is limited for us. It is up to man to know how to manage it well. There is a time for everything, says the Ecclesiastes! If we sow negligence in certain areas of our lives, we will harvest poverty and lack in those specific areas.

Let us be vigilant. Investing only in the church and neglecting your home, will not repair the negative consequences that will come from it. You will have lost your home, you will have failed in the education of your children, etc. Investing in the church and neglecting your job will not give you the financial prosperity you desire. You will have lost your resources.

The Lord loves us. May wisdom be our portion in order to invest in every area of our lives, as it should be.

3. Some examples of different types of life

3.1. The Christian life

This is the fellowship between the children of God, within a local assembly. The only model is the Bible. A church is led by a Senior Pastor, who must equip and train the believers without controlling their private lives. The biblical values are transmitted to us in this way.

Acts 2: 46-47 " *So continuing daily with one accord in the temple, and breaking bread from house to house, they ate their food with gladness and simplicity of heart, 47 praising God and having favor with all the people. And the Lord added to the church daily those who were being saved.*"

3.2. The private spiritual life

This is one's own life of intimacy with the Lord independently from the church, one's spouse, or anyone else. It requires daily solitude in order to pray, worship, meditate, read and study the Word of God, obey the voice of the Lord and listen to Him.

3.3. The family life

Outside of church life, each of us have our respective homes. We all organize ourselves as we see t. God created us with our differences and the church has no business interfering in this area.

If members of the church wish to seek counsel and ask for it themselves, the church may provide it. Counseling does not give one the right to interfere in the private lives of brothers and sisters in the faith. Curiosity is the enemy of community life. We cannot make decisions for the people who con de in us. We must respect each other's decisions and lifestyles even if they do not correspond to ours. We are not allowed to judge our fellow man.

1 Timothy 5:8 *"But if anyone does not provide for his own, and especially for those of his household, he has denied the faith and is worse than an unbeliever."*

3.4. The Professional life

This is my life when I am practicing my profession. I relate to my colleagues in order to achieve the common goal set in the professional framework. We are bound by work.

In this type of relationship, each employee has his or her own beliefs. This diversity does not prevent the work from being done. As long as each others' beliefs are respected, the tasks can be carried out without unnecessary conflicts. This is how Daniel and his friends worked in Babylon, an occultist environment, without having to betray their own faith.

Daniel 6:1-2 *"It pleased Darius to set over the kingdom one hundred and twenty satraps, to be over the whole kingdom; 2 and over these, three governors, of whom Daniel was one, that the satraps might give account to them, so that the king would suffer no loss ..."*

3.5. The social life

This is our relationship with society, with the neighborhood. As Christians, we must respect the established authorities. The Lord asks us to pray for them because our peace largely depends on their decision-making. Respect for authority equally applies to the church. We must respect our church leaders.

Romans 12:18 *"If it is possible, as much as depends on you, live peaceably with all men."*

3.6. Friendships in community life

Do not confuse the fact of living together with being friends.

Just because we belong to the same church community, does not mean that we necessarily must be friends with the people of that congregation. Loving everyone does not mean being friends with everyone. Do not confuse fellowship with friendship.

Ecclesiastes 4:9-10 *Two are better than one, because they have a good reward for their labor. 10 For if they fall, one will lift up his companion. But woe to him who is alone when he falls, for he has no one to help him up.*

N.B.: If we come to respect the different aspects of our lives by being mature, we will avoid many unnecessary conflicts in our assemblies. Let us, therefore, respect the boundaries set by our fellow man and accept each other's differences. Let us avoid always misinterpreting events. To live happily in a community, we must also avoid being curious and wanting to know more about the private lives of the church members.

VII. GUIDE TO RECOGNIZE THE TRUE CHURCH VS CULTS

We are currently witnessing the proliferation of numerous assemblies and prayer groups that are independent of local churches. And many people call themselves pastors or leaders of prayer groups. Many gatherings are held in the name of God. But, are they all really from the Lord?

We must warn you that there are false shepherds and there are false churches. Not all gatherings in the name of God are from God. As we explained earlier, the Lord is a God of order. Many gatherings come from the disorder and are produced by the fleshly nature of man.

Jeremiah 23:20-22 *"The anger of the Lord will not turn back Until He has executed and performed the thoughts of His heart. In the latter days you will understand it perfectly. 21 "I have not sent these prophets, yet they ran. I have not spoken to them, yet they prophesied. 22 But if they had stood in My counsel, And had caused My people to hear My words, Then they would have turned them from their evil way And from the evil of their doings."*

You will need to sincerely pray to the Lord and ask Him to enlighten you, in order to give you a good pastor and a good fixed local church. Your spiritual growth is not a game. The Holy Spirit loves this kind of prayer, and will guide you.

1. The ambitious

While looking for a good congregation, it is important for a Christian to discern ambitious people. These are often people who do not know their own worth and lack self-confidence. They have difficulty submitting to the established authority and can then easily envy the pastoral position. They hope to gain more advantages and consideration by leading an assembly. Thus, they proclaim themselves pastor or leader of a prayer group independent of any church. Untrained and not mandated, they start ministries and make many mistakes.

These pseudo-leaders are not in a position to teach nor to train the people of God. Their activities will therefore mainly revolve around social events and maintaining a certain excitement in prayers. These gatherings cannot last in time and dissolve rather quickly.

We advise you not to be carried away by friendly emotions that will lead you to commit to just any gathering. You never deal with a covenant on the basis of emotions. Always check if the shepherd of an assembly is sufficiently equipped to train you and manage the church. First, check their background and their spiritual mandate.

Proverbs 14:15 *"The simple believes every word, But the prudent considers well his steps."*

Romans 16:18 *"For those who are such do not serve our Lord Jesus Christ, but their own belly, and by smooth words and flattering speech deceive the hearts of the simple."*

Proverbs 20:25 *"It is a snare for a man to devote rashly something as holy, And afterward to reconsider his vows."*

2. The wolves

There are also wolves. The Lord Jesus warned us about them!

2.1. The false prophets

Wolves can be people who do not teach the Word of God, but spend their time predicting the future and giving detailed prophecies about people's lives. Their so-called prophetic message replaces the responsibility that every Christian has to pray and grow personally with the Lord.

This leads to an emotional dependence on these manipulators. You can see that these so-called pastors are failing in their mission as preachers. They give "prophecies" but, do not preach the Word of God. They do not know the Bible and have no interest in speaking about it. The Bible verses that they give are not frequent and often misinterpreted. Whereas, any person called in one of the 5 ministries (apostles, prophet, evangelist, pastor, and teacher) is first of all always a preacher of the Word of God!

These pseudo-prophets do not inspire the fear of God. They do not even have any themselves and practice hypocrisy. These manipulators are people who often worship their own personalities. They easily indulge in debauchery, greed, and all sorts of vices.

Matthew 7:15-16 *"Beware of false prophets, who come to you in sheep's clothing, but inwardly they are ravenous wolves. 16 You will know them by their fruits. Do men gather grapes from thornbushes or figs from thistles?"*

2.2. The false teachers

Wolves can also be what the Bible calls "false teachers." These are pastors who have started well in the faith and in their ministry, who know how to teach, but who have abandoned the Lord along the way! These people no longer fear God and teach doctrines opposed to the Bible!

2 Peter 2:1 *"But there were also false prophets among the people, even as there will be false teachers among you, who will secretly bring in destructive heresies, even denying the Lord who bought them, and bring on themselves swift destruction."*

3. The False Church

A false church is a congregation that has been formed without having been mandated by Christ. It does not fulfill the duties set forth in Ephesians 4.

3.1. The Manipulator

Even if he calls himself a pastor, a manipulator of a false church does in fact not submit to the Word of God. He creates his own doctrine, as opposed to that of the Bible, and places it above it. The doctrines thus taught are not supported by solid Bible verses. Certain sacred texts can be taken out of context and misinterpreted for the sole purpose of defending the manipulator's doctrine.

The cult often revolves around the founder. He does not help the followers to know their ministry and flourish. He does not awaken the thirst to serve and fear God, but rather wants the followers to serve him.

3.2. The pseudo-leaders

In "fake gatherings" often presented under the label of "prayer groups," we find ambitious leaders who like to exercise power over others. What characterizes them, as we have already explained before, is that they are not able to teach and equip the saints. They are not able to help them know their ministry. They also do not know how to manage an assembly. Without a consistent message, this type of group is much more involved in social activities (visits, meals, parties, etc.). The goal is to arouse the emotions of the followers in order to attract them to their meetings.

These so-called "prayer groups" do not last in time because they lack the equipment for true ministry. On the contrary, when God sends a messenger, a shepherd, He gives him a clear message, a clear vision, and a team.

If one is not equipped to manage a group of people, that is for the most part, made up of people with self-fulfilled personalities, spiritual, relational, and even physical abuses arise. These pseudo-leaders act wrongly, because they take believers away from their respective churches to take them nowhere. The believers who follow them, find themselves destabilized and even hurt as a result of the mismanagement of these assemblies. It then becomes di cult for these Christians to return to their former churches.

Having followed a rebel movement, these people end up being lost and wandering, without a fixed church.

3.3. The danger of cults

Cults like to exercise control over their followers, their homes, and their money. The private lives of the members are not well preserved. Sexual aberrations are often present, as well as manipulations. Cults develop a mistrust of the rest of the outside world and tend to demonize and denigrate the work of others.

For the initiators of these groups, God is not at the center of their concern. Only the satisfaction of their fleshly desires concerns them. God's name is only used as bait to gain people's trust. Cults are led by false shepherds. And they often do not respect the rights and properties of members of their congregation.

It is necessary to get out of the grip of cults as quickly as possible. The consequences of this control over the victims are harmful at every level of life: spiritual, emotional, intellectual, relational, material, and physical. They even end up affecting the ability of their followers to make decisions for themselves.

CHAPTER 4
TIMOTHY, A SERVANT OF GOD UNDER PAUL'S AUTHORITY

4

TIMOTHY, A SERVANT OF GOD UNDER PAUL'S AUTHORITY

I. THE EXAMPLE OF TIMOTHY

1. Paul and Timothy

For a better understanding of all that was mentioned in the previous chapter, we will study the example of the servant – Timothy, in the context of the ministry of the apostle Paul. Timothy served the Lord, but not just anyhow. He served God according to the principles laid down in the Bible. Timothy had a clearly identified spiritual father. The Bible shows us that he served God under the authority and the supervision of the apostle Paul.

Paul and Timothy are perfect examples of a good discipleship relationship. Paul was a good teacher and Timothy was a good disciple. We will analyze the qualities of a good servant in light of the stages of Timothy's life: his conversion, his journey, his call, his consecration, his career and his character. His example will be edifying for us.

The Apostle Paul in the Bible repeatedly refers to Timothy as his "spiritual son." This designation shows that it was through Paul's ministry that Timothy truly came to know God and the Apostle Paul was a witness to this.

1Timothy 1:2 *"To Timothy, a true son in the faith: Grace, mercy, and peace from God our Father and Jesus Christ our Lord."*

2Timothy 1:2 *"To Timothy, a beloved son: Grace, mercy, and peace from God the Father and Christ Jesus our Lord."*

1Corinthians 4:17 *"For this reason I have sent Timothy to you, who is my beloved and faithful son in the Lord, who will remind you of my ways in Christ, as I teach everywhere in every church."*

Romans 16:21 *"Timothy, my fellow worker, and Lucius, Jason, and Sosipater, my countrymen, greet you."*

1 Thessalonians 3:2 *"and sent Timothy, our brother and minister of God, and our fellow laborer in the gospel of Christ, to establish you and encourage you concerning your faith,"*

Philippians 1:1 *"Paul and Timothy, bondservants of Jesus Christ, To all the saints in Christ Jesus who are in Philippi, with the bishops and deacons:"*

Philippians 2:19–22 *"But I trust in the Lord Jesus to send Timothy to you shortly, that I also may be encouraged when I know your state. 20 For I have no one likeminded, who will sincerely care for your state. 21 For all seek their own, not the things which are of Christ Jesus. 22 But you know his proven character, that as a son with his father he served with me in the gospel."*

1 Corinthians 16:10 *"And if Timothy comes, see that he may be with you without fear; for he does the work of the Lord, as I also do."*

2. Discipleship is a fundamental part of a Christian journey

When we are reading the Scriptures, we might get the impression that, in comparison to all other disciples, Timothy enjoyed a special privilege from Paul. But, you should know that Paul was not the type to show favoritism. Paul's closeness to Timothy was due to Timothy's commitment, faithfulness, and loyalty. Paul could thus trust him.

The relationship between a teacher and his disciple is necessary in the Christian journey. It must be possible to have this relationship without ever falling into sectarian aberrations. This relationship deserves a good understanding since it will determine the entirety of the exercise of the ministry until the return of the Lord Jesus Christ.

Timothy had a calling as we all do. His was more particularly in the pastoral ministry. Having known his call at a young age, it is interesting to note that he did not rush into opening a church or starting a ministry independently. Nor did he reject or postpone the exercise of his service for God to the future. Rather, he put his gift at the service of his church, under the ministry of the Apostle Paul. He thus took time to be trained and to bene t from Paul's experience.

Unfortunately, many people with pastoral calling are impatient and cannot stand a pastor overseeing their service. Having a call to pastoral ministry is not enough and does not give the right to start a ministry. It is important to put one's gift at the service of one's local church and to enter into a relationship of discipleship with one's teacher. The Lord Jesus Christ Himself first took the time to prepare the apostles before sending them out.

Overriding the authority of the local church family, thinking that you will obtain recognition for your pastoral ministry through Bible school or any other way, is a big mistake! You should know that obtaining a degree in theology does not qualify a person for the 5 ministries! It is the church's task to recognize your ministry and consecrate you.

Every teacher is supposed to have been in the past, a good disciple with a father who was appointed by God. If you have not been a good disciple yourself, it is impossible for you to teach someone how to be one. It is therefore impossible for such people to ever become masters. A master remains a disciple of the Lord Jesus Christ for life. This is how one can render a good service to God until His return.

A servant, who in his exercise has not been serious about the small commitments within his local family, will not go far in his ministry. A man reaps only what he has sown. If we have sown laziness, and negligence, we will reap the fruit of deformity. If we have sown rebellion, we will reap rebellion. If we have sown betrayal, and independence, we will reap betrayal, independence, etc.

We have all witnessed, and perhaps even have been victims of abuse in ministry. These abuses by God's ministers often stem from a bad start in their service. The ministry was misunderstood and started with hidden evil intentions (pride, love of titles, power, the quest for high social status, need for greatness, dominance, making a name for oneself, greed, insubordination, rebellion, etc. rather than serving the true God).

Luke 16:10-12 *"He who is faithful in what is least is faithful also in much; and he who is unjust in what is least is unjust also in much. 11 Therefore if you have not been faithful in the unrighteous mammon, who will commit to your trust the true riches? 12 And if you have not been faithful in what is another man's, who will give you what is your own?"*

II. TIMOTHY'S JOURNEY

So, we will study Timothy's journey of service, which is a good example for us today. This is the journey of a faithful servant. Christ is of course the best model of a servant.

1. The conversion of Timothy

We have explained in chapter 1 of this book, how a person can become a Christian. We have seen that one is not born a Christian, one becomes one. It is impossible to become one by your own strength or e ort. It is only by the power of God. The Christian life, the life of the Spirit, always begins on one particular day. There is always one special day when we repent of our sins and decide to follow Jesus. This is the experience of conversion. This is an essential step that every Christian must have experienced. This also applies to people who were born into a family where the parents were believers and attended church regularly. Faith is not hereditary. God works with a person's will.

The new birth begins by believing in your heart that Jesus died for your sins, and confessing it with your mouth. The servant must know that he has accepted Jesus, not only as his Savior, but also as his Lord and his Master. By believing and confessing, man is thus making a covenant, a pact with God.

Acts 16:1-2 *"Then he came to Derbe and Lystra. And behold, a certain disciple was there, named Timothy, the son of a certain Jewish woman who believed, but his father was Greek. 2 He was well spoken of by the brethren who were at Lystra and Iconium."*

1 Timothy 6:12 *"Fight the good fight of faith, lay hold on eternal life, to which you were also called and have confessed the good confession in the presence of many witnesses."*

During his time, the Apostle Paul witnessed the conversion of Timothy. Timothy was born again and was indeed part of the Worldwide Church of God.

2. The Journey and the testimony of Timothy

Every servant is supposed to have a traceable path.

Melchizedek, King of Salem, who once appeared to Abraham after his victory over Chedorlaomer and the kings who were in alliance with him, is the only one who does not have a genealogy. He is the manifestation of a theophany of God. He is without an ascendant since it was God Himself who appeared to Abraham.

There is no such thing as "Melchizedek servants!" All those whom God has used, had their journey. They all had fathers in the faith, except for a few rare people like Elijah, the Tishbite, described only as one of the inhabitants of Gilead. Beware of servants who cannot present their fathers in the faith! Their feelings are already caught in the nets of rebellion.

Acts 16:1-3 *"Then he came to Derbe and Lystra. And behold, a certain disciple was there, named Timothy, the son of a certain Jewish woman who believed, but his father was Greek. 2 He was well spoken of by the brethren who were at Lystra and Iconium. 3 Paul wanted to have him go on with him. And he took him and circumcised him because of the Jews who were in that region, for they all knew that his father was Greek."*

2 Timothy 1:5 *"when I call to remembrance the genuine faith that is in you, which dwelt first in your grandmother Lois and your mother Eunice, and I am persuaded is in you also."*

3. The calling of Timothy

As we explained in chapter 3, no one can be called to ministry by men or by his own will. The call is divine, and men simply recognize its fruits.

3.1. The call into the ministry is recognized by:

- the inner conviction in your mind;
- the testimony in your heart;
- the spiritual equipment, the gifts of the spirit that accompany the call;
- the outward testimony from others, what people see.

2 Timothy 1:9 *"who has saved us and called us with a holy calling, not according to our works, but according to His own purpose and grace which was given to us in Christ Jesus before time began, …"*

John 15:16 *"You did not choose Me, but I chose you and appointed you that you should go and bear fruit and that your fruit should remain, that whatever you ask the Father in My name He may give you."*

We also suggest you reading Acts 9: the conversion of Saul (the call of the Apostle Paul); and ***Acts 13:1-2***. The Holy Spirit asks that Paul and Barnabas be set apart for the work to which He has called them.

Calling alone is not enough! It is absolutely necessary to add training to your call! The Lord will never send an unprepared worker into the field. He will never send a messenger without a clear message!

3.2. There are 3 different types of training for every Christian and for those who are called to one of the five-fold ministries:

    a.   Spiritual training consists of setting oneself apart under the will of God. It is characterized by an intimate prayer life, the reading of the Word of God, and a life of obedience. These life habits are vital and more important than the position we hold.

John 15:4 *"Abide in Me, and I in you. As the branch cannot bear fruit of itself, unless it abides in the vine, neither can you, unless you abide in me."*

b. Intellectual training. It consists of adding knowledge to faith. We must develop our intellectual capacity, to study the Word of God in depth.

2 Peter 1:5 *"But also for this very reason, giving all diligence, add to your faith virtue, to virtue knowledge,"*

Proverbs 19:2 *"Also it is not good for a soul to be without knowledge, And he sins who hastens with his feet."*

2 Timothy 2:15 *"Be diligent to present yourself approved to God, a worker who does not need to be ashamed, rightly dividing the word of truth."*

c. Practical or technical training. It consists of putting into practice the knowledge acquired during the training courses and being corrected. This allows novices to avoid making mistakes.

Proverbs 12:1 *"Whoever loves instruction loves knowledge, But he who hates correction is stupid."*

Proverbs 13:18 *"Poverty and shame will come to him who disdains correction, But he who regards a rebuke will be honored."*

Proverbs 25:12 *"Like an earring of gold and an ornament of fine gold Is a wise rebuker to an obedient ear."*

1 Timothy 3:6 *"not a novice, lest being puffed up with pride he fall into the same condemnation as the devil."*

4. Consecration / Ordination

Timothy was ordained when he was about 20 years old (see **1Timothy 4:14**). This ceremony took place in agreement with the elders of the local church and by laying on of hands. In this procession, he received the gifts of the Spirit, evidence of divine approval, and equipment for the work.

1 Timothy 1:18 *"This charge I commit to you, son Timothy, according to the prophecies previously made concerning you, that by them you may wage the good warfare,"*

So, Timothy actually received prophecies on several occasions that con rmed his call into the 5 ministries.

1 Timothy 4:14–15 *"Do not neglect the gift that is in you, which was given to you by prophecy with the laying on of the hands of the eldership. 15Meditate on these things; give yourself entirely to them, that your progress may be evident to all."*

5. Career[11]

Timothy did not directly enter the full-time ministry after his ordination. He received the laying on of hands when he was 20 years old. And it was not until the age of 35 that he would minister independently of the Apostle Paul's ministry.

During these 15 transitional years, we see him practicing with the Apostle as:

---

[11] *A. Kuen. "The letters of Paul," Ed. Emmaus 1806 Saint-Légier Switzerland 1982*

- secretary and assistant in the writing of the epistles of the Apostle (act of humility);
- apprentice to the apostle;
- collaborator in the planting of churches in Philippi, Thessalonica, Berea, Corinth, and Ephesus.

He was always there for Paul and supported him in his worst di culties. Timothy continued to help him even when the Apostle was in prison.

Timothy is an example of loyalty and a beautiful example for us today, for those who often want to hurry into ministry without accepting the time of training! This often results in a lot of damage and abuse of all kinds.

Colossians 1:1 *Paul, an apostle of Jesus Christ by the will of God, and Timothy our brother,*

Philippians 1:1 *Paul and Timothy, bondservants of Jesus Christ, To all the saints in Christ Jesus who are in Philippi, with the bishops and deacons:*

Philippians 2:19–22 *"But I trust in the Lord Jesus to send Timothy to you shortly, that I also may be encouraged when I know your state. 20 For I have no one likeminded, who will sincerely care for your state. 21 For all seek their own, not the things which are of Christ Jesus. 22 But you know his proven character, that as a son with his father he served with me in the gospel."*

6. Developing one's character

Note that beyond the information and teachings that we can receive, the difference in what we will accomplish for God will depend largely on our own discipline and obedience to established principles. Fifteen years passed before Timothy fully exercised his ministry. During these years, he had to learn to develop his character. He was thus an exemplary young man for his generation and for us today.

His main weakness was shyness. He accepted that the Apostle Paul worked on his temperament. He did not refuse Paul's injunctions to face the false teachers and prophets. This was very di cult for him. Nevertheless, he refuted and censured them as Paul had asked him to.

Most servants do not complete their training and prefer to leave before their time. They do not measure the risks, demands, and experiences that ministry requires.

1 Samuel 25:10 *"Then Nabal answered David's servants, and said, "Who is David, and who is the son of Jesse? There are many servants nowadays who break away each one from his master."* **1 Timothy 4:12** *"Let no one despise your youth, but be an example to the believers in word, in conduct, in love, in spirit, in faith, in purity."* **1Timothy 5:23** *"No longer drink only water, but use a little wine for your stomach's sake and your frequent infirmities."*

2Timothy 1:6-7 *"Therefore I remind you to stir up the gift of God which is in you through the laying on of my hands. 7 For God has not given us a spirit of fear, but of power and of love and of a sound mind."*

Here is a list of some character traits that a servant should develop just as Timothy did:

6.1. Humility

As Christians, we are all supposed to work on our humility. When you are a shepherd, you must double in vigilance to develop this quality. Indeed, being in a position of authority, the risk of abusing one's power is higher. Accomplishments, experiences, manifestations of the gift of the Spirit, etc., naturally lead man to pride.

1Corinthians 10:12 *"Therefore let him who thinks he stands take heed lest he fall."*

Philippians 2:5,8 *"Let this mind be in you which was also in Christ Jesus ... He humbled Himself and became obedient to the point of death, even the death of the cross."*

6.2. Always seek to be like Christ

We must love to serve rather than to be served. Our model par excellence is Christ. Do not be afraid to make unpopular decisions if they are in accordance with the Word of God.

John 13:14-17 *"If I then, your Lord and Teacher, have washed your feet, you also ought to wash one another's feet. 15 For I have given you an example, that you should do as I have done to you. 16 Most assuredly, I say to you, a servant is not greater than his master; nor is he who is sent greater than he who sent him. 17 If you know these things, blessed are you if you do them."*

6.3. Being modest and simple

As a servant, one must seek to be modest and also to be simple.

Isaiah 14:12-15 *"How you are fallen from heaven, O Lucifer, son of the morning! How you are cut down to the ground, you who weakened the nations! 13 For you have said in your heart: 'I will ascend into heaven, I will exalt my throne above the stars of God; I will also sit on the mount of the congregation on the farthest sides of the north; 14 I will ascend above the heights of the clouds, I will be like the Most High.' 15 Yet you shall be brought down to Sheol, to the lowest depths of the Pit."* (See Isaiah 42)

Luke 20:46 *"Beware of the scribes, who desire to go around in long robes, love greetings in the marketplaces, the best seats in the synagogues, and the best places at feasts, ..."*

6.4. Do not seek recognition from men

You should never work to be appreciated or recognized by men. We are servants of God and not of men! He who lives to be appreciated by humans will betray God. Loving everyone does not mean pleasing everyone. Let us not forget that "all who desire to live godly in Christ Jesus will suffer persecution." "Blessed are you when they revile and persecute you, and say all kinds of evil against you falsely for my sake ...," said Jesus.

Luke 17:9-10 *"Does he thank that servant because he did the things that were commanded him? I think not. 10 So likewise you, when you have done all those things which you are commanded, say, 'We are unprofitable servants. We have done what was our duty to do.'"*

6.5. Accepting the required tasks, even the smallest ones

The servant must accept all tasks, even those that are undervalued.

Because remember, we work for the Kingdom of God. There is thus no minor service!

Romans 12:16 *"Be of the same mind toward one another. Do not set your mind on high things, but associate with the humble. Do not be wise in your own opinion."*

2Samuel 23:15-17 *"And David said with longing, "Oh, that someone would give me a drink of the water from the well of Bethlehem, which is by the gate!" 16 So the three mighty men broke through the camp of the Philistines, drew water from the well of Bethlehem that was by the gate, and took it and brought it to David. Nevertheless he would not drink it, but poured it out to the Lord. 17 And he said, "Far be it from me, O Lord, that I should do this! Is this not the blood of the men who went in jeopardy of their lives?" Therefore he would not drink it."*

2 Kings 3:11 *But Jehoshaphat said, "Is there no prophet of the Lord here that we may inquire of the Lord by him?"*

So one of the servants of the king of Israel answered and said, "Elisha the son of Shaphat is here, who poured water on the hands of Elijah."

6.6. Respect for the elders

Victor Hugo said: "If you look in the eyes of the young, you see the flame. If you look in the eyes of the old, you see light." He was right, we all work in complementarity.

We often tend to ignore the work that was done by our forerunners. Let us not despise the work of the elders in the faith, but rather be attentive and grateful. Let us build on the pre-established foundations. Why destroy or ignore work that has already been done and want to redo everything? It is easier to continue a work that has already been established and thus go further by bringing your stone to the edifice.

Malachi 1:6 *"A son honors his father, and a servant his master. If then I am the Father, Where is my honor? And if I am a Master, Where is my reverence? Says the Lord of hosts to you priests who despise my name. Yet you say, 'In what way have we despised your name?"*

1 Kings 20:11 *So the king of Israel answered and said, "Tell him, 'Let not the one who puts on his armor boast like the one who takes it off."*

CHAPTER 5
DISLOYALTY

5

DISLOYALTY

I. DISLOYALTY AND DIVISION

1. *Beware of disloyalty!*

We are all called to serve God together in our church. And the Lord Jesus warned us that we will be confronted with betrayal and disloyalty. If there is one work that is hated by Satan, it is the Church, the heritage of Christ. And he will attack the visible Church because it is the institution Jesus wanted on earth to organize His service.

The enemy's goal is to divide what God wants to unify. He himself was the first to rebel against the Lord and to form a faction. The Bible calls him the adversary, the opponent, the father of lies. We must not ignore that his spirit of opposing what God has established. is acting on earth.

Division prevents the realization of the mission given by the Lord Jesus, which is making disciples out of Christians. It is an effective weapon for the Prince of this world. Division makes it impossible to form a body in order to achieve the objectives of the church.

We will always have to pray and use wisdom to fight against

disloyalty in our assemblies. Prayer makes us sensitive, it sharpens our spirit. And wisdom is the ability to judge and discern the seeds of rebellion. These two crutches will allow us to act adequately in the face of different circumstances.

1 Samuel 25:33 "And blessed is your advice and blessed are you, because you have kept me this day from coming to bloodshed and from avenging myself with my own hand."

A good servant is supposed to protect the sheepfold to which he belongs, that is, his local church. He must therefore be able to detect the signs of disloyalty. The disciple should not be naive, dreamy or surprised by evil! Being a Christian, and loving your fellow man, does not mean being naive! God does not appreciate naivety at all. On the contrary, we are called to understand how men are. A good servant must be able to anticipate events.

Matthew 10:16 "Behold, I send you out as sheep in the midst of wolves. Therefore be wise as serpents and harmless as doves." Matthew 24:9-10 "Then they will deliver you up to tribulation and kill you, and you will be hated by all nations for My name's sake. 10 And then many will be offended, will betray one another and will hate one another."

The Bible places great emphasis on loyalty. This is the character that allows a group of people to achieve a common goal together.

Therefore, we need to fight against disloyalty by preaching and teaching about it.

The biggest attacks in the sheepfold do not come from the outside, but rather, from the inside. They come from unfaithful men, who are part of the community and who constitute what we can call the *5th column*. These are people who serve as informers or spies, commonly referred to as "wolves in sheep's clothing." They must be detected in order to neutralize their harmful behavior. It is, therefore, necessary to be surrounded by true collaborators in order to preserve the peace of the community.

We want to warn the people of God of these realities and also help to intervene against these destructive behaviors. The goal is to protect ourselves and other members.

We want to remind you that it is a mistake to judge a service as good, solely on the basis of skills. Although it is very important, and even recommended in the Bible, to develop one's abilities, competence is not the cornerstone of the qualities that God looks for in a man. The main quality of a good servant is FAITHFULNESS. To God, an incompetent, but faithful man is better than an unfaithful, but competent man. All the other virtues will come to develop on the basis of faithfulness.

1 Corinthians 4:2 "*Moreover it is required in stewards that one be found faithful.*"

Faithful people will make the work last in time and should be honorably rewarded.

2. Remain vigilant towards oneself

Despite having walked on the path of righteousness, a good servant must always remain vigilant towards himself. He, who is faithful today, may become unfaithful tomorrow if he does not take care of the state of his heart. This is perfectly possible. It is not enough to start well with the Lord, we must above all, finish well, as recommended by Ecclesiastes.

Ecclesiastes 7:8 *"The end of a thing is better than its beginning; The patient in spirit is better than the proud in spirit."*

Proverbs 4:23 *"Keep your heart with all diligence, for out of it spring the issues of life."*

2 Chronicles 26:16 *"But when he was strong his heart was lifted up, to his destruction, for he transgressed against the Lord his God by entering the temple of the Lord to burn incense on the altar of incense."*

Isaiah 14:13 *"For you have said in your heart: 'I will ascend into heaven, I will exalt my throne above the stars of God; I will also sit on the mount of the congregation On the farthest sides of the north;"*

Let us therefore not rely on good past experiences in the faith, but let us watch over our current inner state daily, by the power of the Holy Spirit. It is up to each person to be very careful of their spirit by remaining pure and committed to biblical principles.

3. Characteristics of a rebellion

As a servant belonging to a community, it will be necessary to correct someone at times. This must be done wisely in order to preserve everyone's well-being. That being said, let us not be too quick and simplistic in our judgment of disloyalty. We must be able to differentiate the phenomenon of rebellion from the errors, the weaknesses, and the carnal struggles that are attached to every Christian.

We must also distinguish rebellion from personality disorders (paranoia, schizophrenia, anti-social behavior, borderline disorder, depression, etc.). Indeed, people suffering from personality disorders have difficulties in adapting socially to any environment. What is unique about rebellion is that it aims to destroy a local church. Thus, this is an extremely dangerous evil. Every member of a community must fight against it.

Rebellion is the culmination of unfaithfulness that begins in the heart. It doesn't happen overnight. It is the result of a long process.

Once it has reached its full development, it is almost impossible for such people to turn around; they will take action. Man has reached a point of no return. These people have decided to satisfy their fleshly desires and nothing will stop them.

Rebellion is a conscious decision of man's will. The person has decided to no longer fight against his rebellious tendencies. This is why Jesus said to Judas "whatever you want to do, do it." The unrevealed feeling that drives a rebellious person is envy, which is di cult to admit.

This was the case of Judas towards Jesus, of Absalom towards his father, King David, of Cain towards his brother, Abel, among others.

Note that these people never repented of their bad deeds and never wanted to work on the envious state of their hearts. Even though you multiply love for them, they will never be satisfied.

Disloyal people should not be treated with pity because their dangerousness could bring down the edifice at any time. It often takes time before their true intentions are clearly revealed.

1 Timothy 5:24 *"Some men's sins are clearly evident, preceding them to judgment, but those of some men follow later."*

4. What to do when facing rebellion

You will have no other choice, but to drive out the rebels. Do not confuse love with discipline. Discipline is part of love. The church works by discipline. If this is not done wisely, the local church cannot stand.

Proverbs 22:10 *"Cast out the scoffer, and contention will leave; Yes, strife and reproach will cease."*

Proverbs 26:20 *"Where there is no wood, the fire goes out; And where there is no talebearer, strife ceases."*

Matthew 12:30 *"He who is not with me is against me, and he who does not gather with me scatters abroad."*

II. THE STAGES OF REBELLION12

As we study disloyalty in the Bible, we can see that similar cases emerge in almost all the biblical accounts. For this study, we recommend reading the book of 2 Samuel chapters 13 to 16, and advise you to make conclusions. These passages tell us the story of the rebellion of Absalom, the son of king David, against his own father, king David.

In this chapter, we will study the different stages of disloyalty that lead to rebellion. This will allow us to better guard our own hearts, to act firmly and more adequately against these attacks in order to preserve the community.

1. A bad autonomy or an independent spirit

A person who is a part of a community like a local church, should not develop what we call "bad autonomy" or "independent spirit." It is an attitude that pushes one to wanting to stand out, by doing things differently from the group without respecting the principles of the community vision. As Christians, it is not enough to serve with good personal intentions. Rather, we must develop good intentions according to principles that are already established.

An independent spirit, in the sense of non-compliance to instructions, is a bad seed. It is possible to be present in an assembly without submitting to the rules. These people will tend to do the opposite of what is done, with questions like "Why a meeting at 4 p.m.? Why on a Thursday?," and the likes. They often hide their true independent intentions by refusing

---

12 *Inspired by the book of D.H. Mills "loyalty and disloyalty" Parchment House 2017*

to follow the direction of the group under the pretext of "I am spiritual" or "the Spirit told me to do this."

2 Samuel 3: 20-21; 26-27 20 *"So Abner and twenty men with him came to David at Hebron. And David made a feast for Abner and the men who were with him. 21 Then Abner said to David, "I will arise and go, and gather all Israel to my lord the king, that they may make a covenant with you, and that you may reign over all that your heart desires." So David sent Abner away, and he went in peace. 26 And when Joab had gone from David's presence, he sent messengers after Abner, who brought him back from the well of Sirah. But David did not know it. 27 Now when Abner had returned to Hebron, Joab took him aside in the gate to speak with him privately, and there stabbed him in the stomach so that he died for the blood of Asahel his brother."*

2 Samuel 18: 5, 12, 14 *5 Now the king had commanded Joab, Abishai, and Ittai, saying, "Deal gently for my sake with the young man Absalom." And all the people heard when the king gave all the captains orders concerning Absalom. 12 But the man said to Joab, "Though I were to receive a thousand shekels of silver in my hand, I would not raise my hand against the king's son. For in our hearing the king commanded you and Abishai and Ittai, saying, 'Beware lest anyone touch the young man Absalom!' 14 Then Joab said, "I cannot linger with you." And he took three spears in his hand and thrust them through Absalom's heart, while he was still alive in the midst of the terebinth tree.*

2. The offense (unhealed wounds)

In any relationship, conflicts can arise from time to time. This is why fellowship with others requires maturity. A good servant must be able to handle disagreements. My fellow man being is different from me; misunderstandings are inevitable at times. Understanding this is a matter of maturity. Maturity can be summed up as accepting oneself, asserting oneself, and remaining oneself in the community. This is an attitude you learn and develop with time.

When people are hurt, or o ended for several reasons, they can start to develop negative and separatist thoughts such as: "I am not useful here," "Andrew was chosen in such office and not me," et cetera. They will be focused on small details and interpret them negatively without seeking to obtain clear explanations of the situation at hand. When we are hurt, we must not let the enemy win our hearts by drawing our own conclusions too quickly. Beliefs that grow out of hurt and bitterness are often wrong. Unresolved hurt feelings develop hatred and translate into anger.

Unfortunately, these feelings will always be directed towards the person in charge.

N.B.: *Let us be very careful with hurt people, they often become traitors.*

Take the example of Absalom's rebellion. Amnon, Absalom's halfbrother raped his half-sister, Absalom's sister. King David spares his son, Amnon, from the death penalty (normally imposed for this kind of crime). The consequence of this granted favor deeply hurts Absalom, who feels dishonored. David protected his son Amnon, whereas the law stipulated stoning for such an offense.

It is understandable that as a father, king David did not want his son Amnon to be stoned. But, he still should have tried to solve this problem in another way. He, for example, could have punished Amnon with a less severe punishment than death, and helped Absalom recover from this hurt. We see in this account that king David did not deal with the root of this problem. He did nothing about it and let time pass. Unfortunately, without proper treatment, time does not heal such wounds. The result was a rebellion that was di cult to stop.

3. Indifference or passivity

When one is o ended, whether it is justified or not, the attitude taken will reveal the maturity or immaturity of the servant. People with weak personalities react to a problem by running away or by manipulation. They prefer not to face difficulties. They choose to ignore them and show indifference or passivity within the group. Indifference can manifest itself in not showing up for meetings or church activities, not responding to emails, not answering the phone, not returning calls, etc.

This is a strong signal about your leadership. It is a threat and a challenge, a way of sending you a message of dissatisfaction.

Pay close attention to passive or indifferent people in the group. You have to identify them. They often develop complaints like: "They did …, they abandoned me, they always choose …, they did not understand that …," etc.

2 Samuel 13:22,28 22 "And Absalom spoke to his brother Amnon neither good nor bad. For Absalom hated Amnon because he had forced his sister Tamar. 28 Now Absalom had commanded his servants, saying, "Watch now, when Amnon's heart is merry with wine, and when I say to you, 'Strike Amnon!' then kill him. Do not be afraid. Have I not commanded you? Be courageous and valiant. Jeremiah

48:10 Cursed is he who does the work of the Lord deceitfully, And cursed is he who keeps back his sword from blood."

4. Negative judgment or critical thinking

Criticism is the action of reproaching or blaming someone by only pointing out the faults and errors of this person. This type of criticism is negative and not constructive. It simply aims to denigrate, devalue, and make a person feel guilty.

Constructive criticism consists of analyzing, examining, and sharing actual facts with respect to others, and aims to advance the work.

At this stage, the rebellious person continues to amplify the mistakes. A popular saying tells us that, "he who does nothing only finds remarks to make." Criticism is a seed that breaks love, creates suspicion, destroys the sheepfold, and divides. Keep in mind that, some remarks are often made by critics: "they are not well organized," "the service lacks excellence," "our money is misused," "the leaders are not up to the task," "this church does not visit people," "people are not assisted enough," "they don't call me enough," etc.

Note that in any criticism related to the local church, the person really targeted is the shepherd of the congregation and/or the heads of the various departments.

Matthew 25:24 *"Then he who had received the one talent came and said, 'Lord, I knew you to be a hard man, reaping where you have not sown, and gathering where you have not scattered seed."* **Judges 21:25**

"In those days there was no king in Israel; everyone did what was right in his own eyes."

Matthew 26:31 *"Then Jesus said to them, "All of you will be made to stumble because of me this night, for it is written: 'I will strike the Shepherd, and the sheep of the flock will be scattered."*

It is important for a servant of God to exercise authority without discrimination. We must act and stop the criticism. If they are made in public, they must be corrected in public in order to assert your authority. It must be done without going to war with someone, by using wisdom and discernment to avoid fueling the re. Above all, do not cover up or bury a problem that could destroy your assembly with a false definition of love. Such an approach is a sign of weakness and lack of authority.

***Proverbs 26:4*-5** *"Do not answer a fool according to his folly, Lest you also be like him. 5 Answer a fool according to his folly, lest he be wise in his own eyes."*

Proverbs teaches us to know when to act and when not to act.

Beloved in the Lord, take heed. Let us not turn our houses into "cursed houses," where people come to talk about the evil of the church with anecdotes such as: "What do you think? What do you see? Don't you nd that? We're tired of telling that man, your leader, the same thing." "Really, your daddy is exaggerating, did you hear what he said again, your leader?" etc.

2 Samuel 15:3 *"Then Absalom would say to him, "Look, your case is good and right; but there is no deputy of the king to hear you."*

5. Discerning diplomacy or politics

The rebels that we qualify as "politicians," usually say things people like to hear in order to gain their trust and accomplish their personal goals. Do not trust what they say.

John 2:24 *"But Jesus did not commit Himself to them, because He knew all men, …"*

Politician-rebels always trick naïve people into adhering to their ideologies. In politics, truth is a weapon used to manipulate or to please, in order to achieve one's ends.

- Here are some examples of the tricks used by the politician-rebels:
- "Let us pray a lot for our Pastor so that he should not be weak towards women." This implies that the Pastor might be weak towards certain women.
- The trust in that man of God thus disappears;
- "Let us pray a lot for our heads of departments so that they should be competent." This is a criticism that implies that they are not competent and which devalues the concerned;
- "The Pastor has started to travel a lot, we must be sure that he does not have another commitment";
- "Don't you see that the number of people in the church is decreasing, what is really happening in private? Is the Pastor still praying? ;
- "The pastor has changed a lot, he no longer has time for us since he bought his new house"; etc.

Proverbs 1:10-11 " *My son, if sinners entice you, Do not consent. 11 If they say, "Come with us, Let us lie in wait to shed blood; Let us lurk secretly for the innocent without cause;"*

At this stage of rebellion, negative reports keep coming: "Everyone is saying this or that," etc. A good servant must quickly act and stop these criticisms, because the sheepfold is burning. Complaints and detractions are not bourne out of love! Where are all these complaints leading us? Let us not be manipulated. Let us open our eyes and ask the detractors to be clear with their "everyone is saying that" statements. Ask them more specific questions such as "who are those who say?" Call people in order to confront them. We cannot make a judgment on the basis of a single testimony.

Exodus 23:1-2 *"You shall not circulate a false report. Do not put your hand with the wicked to be an unrighteous witness. 2 You shall not follow a crowd to do evil; nor shall you testify in a dispute so as to turn aside after many to pervert justice."*

6. Deviation, misappropriation, or seduction

It is important not to be seduced by rebellion. The rebels will never reveal their true intentions. They will always use trickery and manipulation in order to get their way. A good member must be able to identify the deviations and seductions that are being employed.

6.1. Examples of seduction

One day, Aaron and Mariam rebelled against their own brother,

Moses. They used seduction and trickery to divert the people of God from the authority of their shepherd. They put forward the excuse of his marriage to a foreign woman of Ethiopian origin, in order to turn the assembly against the leadership of Moses. But behind this mask, were their true intentions:

Numbers 12:2 *So they said, "Has the Lord indeed spoken only through Moses? Has He not spoken through us also" And the Lord heard it.*

Here is another example of words spoken during the revolt of Korah, Dathan and Abiram against Moses:

Numbers 16:3 *They gathered together against Moses and Aaron, and said to them, "You take too much upon yourselves, for all the congregation is holy, every one of them, and the Lord is among them. Why then do you exalt yourselves above the assembly of the Lord?"*

It is easier to manipulate people with little education and those who do not have strong personalities. These people find it di cult to deal with the impasse and to question the information they receive. Unfortunately, for many people, the mere fact that they are being confronted by a group of two or three people is enough for them to give in. They will betray their values and even the people who are close to them.

6.2. Excellence does not allow rebellion

In the service that we offer to God, we can also be seduced when we think that we are better than our superior.

A son can do better than his father, but will always remain his father's son. One is a son to his father for life. A good father always wants his son to do more than he has done. Likewise, the Lord Jesus wants us to do greater things than He did. This is perfectly possible. But, even if we do, let us not fall into the trap of pride and think that we have become God. The fact that we are not God does not devalue us in any way.

John 14:12 *"Most assuredly, I say to you, he who believes in me, the works that I do he will do also; and greater works than these he will do, because I go to My Father."*

Let us, therefore, understand that among us, and as members of His body, we are complementary.

Former United States President, Donald Trump, inherited his parents' fortune. He innovated and multiplied their wealth. Although he did more than his father, he is not greater than his elders. When we are seduced, we develop thoughts like: "I lead a community that has more people than my father," "I win more souls than him, I have achieved more than him," "I have built a bigger temple than his," etc.

1 Kings 20:11-12 *So the king of Israel answered and said, "Tell him, 'Let not the one who puts on his armor boast like the one who takes it off.' " 12 And it happened when Ben-Hadad heard this message, as he and the kings were drinking at the command post, that he said to his servants, "Get ready." And they got ready to attack the city.*

John 13:16 *"Most assuredly, I say to you, a servant is not greater than his master; nor is he who is sent greater than he who sent him."*

Ezekiel 28:14,17 14 *"You were the anointed cherub who covers; I established you; You were on the holy mountain of God; You walked back and forth in the midst of fiery stones (...) 17 "Your heart was lifted up because of your beauty; You corrupted your wisdom for the sake of* *your splendor; I cast you to the ground, I laid you before kings, That they might gaze at you."*

6.3. Excellence for a well-functioning team

God does not only speak to the Pastor. He speaks to everyone. Each person has his or her intimacy with Him. The Lord speaks in dierent ways. He can also speak to the Pastor through revelations that the believers have received.

When you receive revelations from the Lord, it is important to realize that within the local church, God has established an order of service. The believers cannot make decisions and take action without going through their Pastor, even when God has spoken to them. They must inform the shepherd about the revelations, visions, and plans they have at heart for their church. The goal is to ensure the proper functioning of the assembly.

As explained in chapter 3, the role of a pastor is to coordinate all the services and gifts within his congregation. It is the Pastor who makes decisions in the church. He is the one who will give or will not give the mandate for the accomplishment of a particular mission. The Pastor will appreciate the zeal, the creativity, the innovation and the revelations brought by a Christian. As explained in chapter 3, the purpose of pastoral work is to make a member active and proactive in his or her field. Passivity and lack of initiative are not at all appreciated in a church. While remaining proactive, members must understand that their actions are part of a collective dynamic. Collaboration, communication, and respect for hierarchies are absolutely necessary for the realization of effective team service.

The church, like any institution, operates according to an established order, according to a discipline. No institution can function without hierarchy. Going against the authority is destructive to an organization. Even if we have good intentions, this motive is not enough. Good intentions are not enough. It is necessary to have good intentions that you can apply through good principles.

7. Revolution or taking action

Once a person's mind and will have crossed all the points listed above, nothing can stop a rebellious person from taking action. The open rebellion then begins. This is the execution stage; the stage where the person takes action. He has become openly and extremely arrogant and boastful. Accusations and convictions abound. You hear phrases like: "you said this about someone, and that about another," "don't forget that I know everything you are doing," "you forgot what you said to André," etc. In this phase, the descent to hell has begun. The great destruction is engaged.

Revelations 12:7 *And war broke out in heaven: Michael and his angels fought with the dragon; and the dragon and his angels fought, …*

2 Samuel 16:11,22 *And David said to Abishai and all his servants, "See how my son who came from my own body seeks my life. How much more now may this Benjamite? Let him alone, and let him curse; for so the Lord has ordered him (…) 22 So they pitched a tent for Absalom on the top of the house, and Absalom went in to his father's concubines in the sight of all Israel.*

Matthew 26:47-48 And while He was still speaking, behold, Judas, one of the twelve, with a great multitude with swords and clubs, came from the chief priests and elders of the people. 48 Now His betrayer had given them a sign, saying, "whomever I kiss, He is the One; seize Him."

III. THE CONSEQUENCES OF A REBELLION

When we read the Bible, we can see that the lives of all the men who needlessly rebelled against the work of God or against established authority, ended badly. The consequences of a rebellion are always negative. They range from simple judgments to the worst diseases, madness and even death. Let us, therefore, be careful to not participate in it, but to fight against it.

Let us consider some biblical examples of the judgments that came upon some rebels:

1. Satan, former head of worship in heaven

Revelations 12:9 So the great dragon was cast out, that serpent of old, called the Devil and Satan, who deceives the whole world; he was cast to the earth, and his angels were cast out with him.

In the example of Satan, we can see that he envied God and wanted to be worshiped in His place. Satan's rebellion caused his downfall. God rejected him and the ⅓ of all the angels who supported him. They were all cast down and became fallen angels.

2. Absalom, son of David

2 Samuel 18:15 *And ten young men who bore Joab's armor surrounded Absalom, and struck and killed him.*

Absalom was o ended by Amnon who rapcd his sister. He must have felt betrayed by his father, king David, when he did not apply the penalty of stoning prescribed by the law, against Amnon. He ended up taking revenge by killing his half-brother, Amnon. Absalom's anger and pain were well-justified, one would say. However, this did not give him the right to rebel against his father, the king, and to want to take his place and attempt to assassinate him. By doing so, he was no longer taking revenge for Amnon's offense, but instead, he was rebelling against God and against the one whom God had established as king.

Absalom's life, like all rebels, ended badly. Even though king David had given formal instructions to his generals to arrest Absalom and not kill him, Absalom was put to death as he ed.

3. Ahithophel, David's counselor

2 Samuel 17:23 *Now when Ahithophel saw that his advice was not followed, he saddled a donkey, and arose and went home to his house, to his city. Then he put his household in order, and hanged himself, and died; and he was buried in his father's tomb.*

Ahithophel was king David's counselor. He betrayed him by supporting Absalom's rebellion. He then became his advisor. His act of rebellion ended up leading him to madness and delirium. He ended up killing himself.

King Nebuchadnezzar and king Saul are also examples of people who became insane for opposing God. God withdraws His presence from them and madness invades the empty heart of man. Nebuchadnezzar was stricken with lycanthropy. This is a psychiatric disease in which the patient believes he has transformed into an animal.

4. Shimei, David's enemy

1 Kings 2:25,46 So King Solomon sent by the hand of Benaiah the son of Jehoiada; and he struck him down, and he died (...) 46 So the king commanded Benaiah the son of Jehoiada; and he went out and struck him down, and he died. Thus the kingdom was established in the hand of Solomon.

Time does not spare the rebels if they do not show true repentance. This is the case of Shimei, who showed rebellion against king David when he was fleeing from his own son, Absalom. During the king's lifetime, Shimei never paid for the wrong he had done. It was king David's son, Solomon, who struck him.

5. Judas, companion of Jesus

Matthew 27:5 Then he threw down the pieces of silver in the temple and departed, and went and hanged himself.

Acts 1:18-19 Now this man purchased a field with the wages of iniquity; and falling headlong, he burst open in the middle and all his entrails gushed out. 19And it became known to all those dwelling in

Jerusalem; so that field is called in their own language, AkelDama, that is, Field of Blood.) ...

The Bible tells us that Judas returned the money he had been given to betray Jesus. This is an act that may seem good at rst sight. Unfortunately, it is not the case in the eyes of God, because Judas did not repent! Do not confuse guilt with repentance! Judas preferred to die rather than repent. He acted differently from Peter who had also betrayed Jesus, but had repented of his act. He was thus able to continue his walk with God.

How hardened is the heart of a rebel! Rebellion leads us away from the path of grace and favor. It eventually destroys a person's judgment. Judas had lost all divine security. So much so that when he wanted to hang himself, the branch of the tree to which he had attached himself broke and he fell. His entrails gushed out.

Many people, like Judas, think that if they rebel somewhere, they will always find refuge elsewhere. This is a mistake. He who destroys God's work will meet the Lord wherever he goes. This was the case with the prophet Jonah who ended up saying to God,

"where shall I flee from Your presence?"

6. Reffection and call to repentance

Beloved in the Lord, God loves you. Let us be careful with ourselves. Rebellion must be understood as a very dangerous virus from which we must protect ourselves. Let us keep our hearts pure, by staying away from rebellious people, who destroy churches. Let us remember Korah's rebellion in the desert against Moses. What was the fate of Korah and the people who followed him? The consequences can be irreversible. Let us not become opponents of God because no one can wage war against Him and win. As long as it depends on us, as the book of Romans recommends us, live in peace with all men.

If by reading this chapter, you recognize that you have participated in one way or another in the division of an assembly, we recommend that you take the time to repent before the Lord and that you repair the damage caused to the church and the Pastor concerned.

IV. HOW TO LOYALLY LEAVE A FAMILY

As explained at the beginning of this book, when we receive the salvation of Jesus Christ, we have agreed to become His "doulos," His servants. The perfect will of God is that we serve Him according to biblical principles. The Scriptures show us that the Lord wants every Christian to serve God in His local church.

The assembly that led you to salvation and/or discipled you, has undeniably been a source of blessing to you. If for any reason, you wish to leave them, it is essential to do so with mutual respect, good understanding and preferably according to biblical principles.

Romans 12:18 *If it is possible, as much as depends on you, live peaceably with all men.*

Let us not forget that we are doing God's work and that the local church-sheepfold must in no case become the stage for our personal ambitions! The church does not belong to the Pastor, but to the Lord Jesus Christ, who hired the Pastor. The departure must be done in peace, in order to avoid leaving behind relational damage.

1. The procedure

It is important to begin by clearly informing the head Pastor of your intention to leave the congregation. Avoid talking about it to the members of the church, it will upset them. It is up to the Pastor to inform them. If you start by talking about it to friends or congregants, you will create ambiguity and this will lead to a spiral of unmanageable interpretations for the congregation.

Community life requires trust and good communication.

Anything vague and ambiguous is close to darkness, disrupts relationships, and will automatically be seen as disloyal behavior. Never leave a congregation without making sure that you have established good, clear, and respectful communication with the institution about your wanting to leave. Work out the details of your departure with the Pastor, especially if you were very involved or responsible for a department.

As a Christian, it is important for you to leave by keeping the peace and seeking the blessing of your church. From the point of view of the local church, you should know that if the church counted on you and trained you, your departure, even if legitimate, is disabling and will not leave anyone indifferent. A decision to leave is always shocking for the party that did not expect it. It will take some time to accept this new situation. This is why you will have to communicate as well as possible and seek peace. The community will need to know, through its Pastor, the reasons for you leaving in order to be at ease.

When the departure is properly planned and well-managed, it will be accepted by all. The congregation might even warmly celebrate it, which will be a good beginning for your future Christian walk without them.

Luke 15:12–13 *And the younger of them said to his father, 'Father, give me the portion of goods that falls to me.' So he divided to them his livelihood. 13 And not many days after, the younger son gathered all together, journeyed to a far country, and there wasted his possessions with prodigal living.*

2. Valid reasons

According to the Bible, there are three valid reasons for a Christian to leave a congregation:

2.1. False doctrines

We are biblically entitled to leave a church when we find that the fundamental doctrines taught by the Pastor are opposed to the Word of God. We must then first try to speak about this problem to the leader of the assembly with love.

This approach is recommended to us in the Scriptures: "in order to bring his brother, his sister back to the right path." Make your position clear with respect to their beliefs and your differences. Do not be ambiguous about your position. Be truthful, sincere, and clear in your approach. Do not compromise. It is possible to be respectful without betraying yourself. Remember that it is your right to look for an assembly that corresponds to you as a Christian.

If despite your many e orts to advise the leader, you do not notice any change, you have the right to leave and pray to the Lord to guide you to find a church that submits to the Word of God.

When you leave, you should continue to respect this church, even if you do not agree with their movement. Avoid gossip and defamation. Avoid turning some members against their direction. Go your own way and leave peacefully. Simply and clearly state your own convictions.

2.2. Misbehavior of the head Pastor

We are also biblically entitled to leave a church when the Pastor behaves immorally. Faced with this situation, you will first try to find him privately and lovingly talk to him about it. If despite these steps, you do not notice any change, you have the right to leave this congregation. If the Pastor is a manipulator, you are likely to encounter opposition and conflict. Pray to the Lord and maintain your position. As long as it depends on you, keep the peace. We remind you that it is your right to look for a church that suits you as a Christian.

2.3. New work desired by God

One can also leave a congregation when the Lord clearly asks for it. This was for example the case of Paul and Barnabas in *Acts 13:2-3.*

Acts 13:2-3 As they ministered to the Lord and fasted, the Holy Spirit said, "Now separate to Me Barnabas and Saul for the work to which I have called them." 3 Then, having fasted and prayed, and laid hands on them, they sent them away.

Please, note that when the Lord speaks thus in public, He confirms His message in the hearts of several other members of the assembly. When God issues such a request, everything always happens in a harmonious manner, without vagueness or ambiguity. God is a God of order and peace. The Lord will never speak to divide His church. This type of departure does not destroy a community since it is a new mission that the Lord entrusts to someone.

3. Other non-biblical reasons

It is also possible that a Christian wants to leave his church for reasons other than those previously mentioned. There are many reasons: relocation, cultural reasons, language differences, discomfort, difficulty in practicing as one desires, etc.

It is always important to talk to your Pastor beforehand about these concerns. This will allow the church to become aware of them and try to organize things in order to make up for any shortcomings. It is possible that as a human being, not knowing everything, your Pastor may have missed some elements. Talking about your discomfort or some shortcomings you have noticed, can help improve communication, collaboration, and work.

The Pastor can then try to improve your integration within the community or direct you to an assembly that might be better suited for you, if you so wish.

4. *Biblically invalid reasons*

Biblically, invalid reasons for wanting to leave a local congregation are purely carnal ones, such as: following a rebellion, personal ambitions, wanting to start one's own church, the quest to obtain higher social status, or a need to proclaim oneself a pastor, as a result of debauchery, adultery, quarrels, jealousy, envy towards the property of others, not being able to bear the blessing of one's brother or sister in Christ, greed, laziness, negligence, wickedness, etc. These reasons are not validated by the Bible.

However, if it should become impossible for you to continue to attend your assembly for reasons that are personal to you, know that you are free to serve God. God does not force anyone, but always acts with the will of man. Nevertheless, we must warn you about the pitfalls you may encounter.

Ending your involvement with your local church will not take away your salvation. You are still a Christian. However, this position is dangerous for your walk, because abandoning your congregation is not the perfect will of God. It is even a sin. You are putting yourself in a risky position that could drag you very far from the Lord.

No church is perfect. No relationship is free from conflict. Only in fellowship do we learn to love and deal with differences. Leaving the church in order to avoid this type of confrontation will not help your Christian growth. Moving to another church is not the real solution. You will face the same tests, the same trials, and the same problems until you learn to overcome them.

Let us accept this biblical truth which informs us that man is a sinner and that he needs to be regularly purified by the blood of the Lord Jesus Christ. Let us dare to face our fleshly desires which are di cult to admit. Let us face them in the light of the Word of God. The Lord gave us the Holy Spirit to give us victory over the flesh. This victory can only be obtained when we stop denying the evidence of the sin that lives within us and accept that the Lord is doing a great work in our hearts. The Lord only works through repentance. Repentance is only possible when man stops blaming others and accepts to see what is wrong in him. He then takes his responsibilities in all circumstances and thus grows spiritually.

5. Disagreements

If you think that you can start a work, a mission, know that this is done according to the order already established in the Bible. There is a whole procedure as detailed in Timothy's example in chapter 4 of this book. God, not being a God of disorder, the Holy Spirit will also warn the leading Pastor and other members of the community of this new call.

If it happens that your feelings are not recognized by the Pastor and by the community, know that you cannot force anyone to follow you. If you are convinced that God has spoken to you, but they are convinced that God has not spoken to them, you will have to make your own decision.

In such circumstances, do not rebel. Do not scandalize your assembly. Make your intentions clear to the Pastor. Do not try to divide the church and turn some members against their leader in order to begin your work with them. Remember that rebellion always has negative consequences.

Do not tell the members of the congregation that you wish to leave, but communicate it to the Pastor. He will make the o cial announcement. Do not slander or smear the reputation of the Pastor and other members in order to make yourself look good.

Prepare your departure in peace. If God has asked you to leave, you have nothing to fear, He will take care of you. Go in peace and bless your former church.

In order to avoid hurt and damage, several Pastors, including Pastor Dag Heward, recommend a waiting period of a few months to a year between the period when one has made one's intention to leave known and the time that one officially leaves. The length of time depends on the importance of the responsibilities that one had within the assembly and the threshold of endurance of this waiting period for the person who wishes to leave. It is even possible in our disagreements to step away by leaving peace in the community. There are many solutions.

Biblical examples of disagreements

The Bible is full of examples of disagreements. Some people have managed to handle them in a Christian way.

This was the case for Abraham and Lot, Paul and Barnabas, Paul and the apostles who doubted his message in Jerusalem, etc.

We can read the example of the disagreement between Paul and Barnabas in *Acts 15:39*. They had a sharp disagreement concerning John Mark, Barnabas' cousin. The Apostle Paul refused to take him with them as a mission worker because he had abandoned them in the past. Barnabas, on the other hand, still wanted him to accompany them. Paul and Barnabas, not agreeing on this subject ended up parting ways. They did so without tarnishing their respective reputations. Barnabas went to work with his cousin. And Paul went his own way.

In *2 Timothy 4:11*, long after these events, when the Apostle Paul was imprisoned, he asked for John Mark to be with him, because he recognized his value.

The history of the Bible is dotted with numerous councils: the Council of Nicaea in 325, the Council of Constantinople in 381, the Council of Ephesus in 431, the Council of Chalcedon in 451, etc. The need to establish councils demonstrates that there were many disagreements and that Christians needed to find common grounds.

Disagreements in themselves are not bad. They are even necessary. It is how we handle our disagreements that matter. We cannot judge or blame a person for what God may or may not have said to them. But, we can judge how we ourselves react to conflicts; if we handle them with Christian maturity or not.

Let us take responsibility for our decisions and not make the church and people weak in the faith become victims of our immature and carnal actions.

CHAPTER 6
MATURITY

6

Maturity

I. THE DEFINITION OF MATURITY

The goal of spiritual growth, as described in Ephesians 4, is to achieve "the stature of maturity." It is a spiritual and psychological state that has reached the fullness of its development. Man is able to judge. He is willing to take responsibility and manifest Christ through his conduct. This is what the Bible calls "the mature state" as opposed to "the childlike state."

Ephesians 4:12–14 *"for the equipping of the saints for the work of ministry, for the edifying of the body of Christ, 13 till we all come to the unity of the faith and of the knowledge of the Son of God, to a perfect man, to the measure of the stature of the fullness of Christ; 14 that we should no longer be children, tossed to and fro and carried about with every wind of doctrine, by the trickery of men, in the cunning craftiness of deceitful plotting, …"*

We are all called to grow, because life without progress is not desirable or any good. As a Christian, we must grow to be like Christ.

The Greek word for maturity is "teleiotes," with its other declensions like "telesphoreo," which means to lead to perfection, to bear fruit at maturity, to be complete, to become adult, resistant, and stable. The objective is therefore to be an adult to the point of enlisting, of assuming one's responsibilities. This is the goal that the servant of God must aim for.

To remain a child means to be under someone's guardianship, to still be dependent. The Latin word for child is "infantem" from "infans," which means the one who does not have a word to say, who does not have enough will; in other words, the one whom you always have to defend.

Galatians 4:1 "*Now I say that the heir, as long as he is a child, does not differ at all from a slave, though he is master of all, …*"

The Lord wants us to become sons and daughters that are able to take care of His work. As already mentioned, true maturity is being like Christ. But, no human being can get to that perfection because it is infinite. But, that does not exempt us from bearing fruits. This is why it is better to see maturity as being on "a lifelong journey."

Maturity can therefore be considered as a fruit when it is ripe. The seed dies and grows to become this plant organ. Just as the fruit is visible, appreciated and consumable, so can we see the actions of a mature man and those around him bene t from it.

II. THE MANIFESTATION OF MATURITY

The mature servant understands the notions of "me," "you," "him" and "us." He understands that the sheepfold is made up of different kinds of sheep. He is able to balance this reality.

Maturity also manifests itself within the sheepfold by understanding the concepts of complementarity, teamwork, the acceptance of similarities and differences within a community, and controlling one's emotions. And this is opposed to competition, fear, feeing and other negative reactions.

Knowing that maturity is visible as a fruit, we can therefore see it by our way of acknowledging others, appreciating them, encouraging them, supporting them. If we find it di cult to do this, it is because a great amount of personal work still needs to be done within us.

Isaiah 41:6 Everyone helped his neighbor, And said to his brother, "Be of good courage!

When we show this behavior that we call "maturity" like a fruit that has reached its fullness, we can be consumed, which means, to occupy positions of responsibilities.

Luke 6:40 A disciple is not above his teacher, but everyone who is perfectly trained will be like his teacher.

Reaching the stage of maturity does not depend on age. One can develop maturity at any age, just as one can at any age remain in the "childlike state." To give responsibilities to "a child" is to destroy the work in advance. The Bible says, woe to the nation for whom the king is a child!

Ecclesiastes 10:16-17 *Woe to you, O land, when your king is a child, and your princes feast in the morning! 17 Blessed are you, O land, when your king is the son of nobles, and your princes feast at the proper time— For strength and not for drunkenness!*

Isaiah 3:4-5 *"I will give children to be their princes, and babes shall rule over them. 5 The people will be oppressed, every one by another and every one by his neighbor; the child will be insolent toward the elder, and the base toward the honorable."*

Maturity is not measured by the knowledge acquired (through Bible school or otherwise) or by the success of certain achievements. Nor is it measured by the number of years spent in the Christian walk. Rather, it has to do with how we live, how we manifest our Christian character, namely the development of the fruit of the Spirit.

Galatians 5:22-23 *"But the fruit of the Spirit is love, joy, peace, longsuffering, kindness, goodness, faithfulness, 23. gentleness, selfcontrol. Against such there is no law."*

Galatians 5:19-21 *Now the works of the flesh are evident, which are: adultery, fornication, uncleanness, lewdness, 20 idolatry, sorcery, hatred, contentions, jealousies, outbursts of wrath, selfish ambitions, dissensions, heresies, 21 envy, murders, drunkenness, revelries, and the like; of which I tell you beforehand, just as I also told you in time past, that those who practice such things will not inherit the kingdom of God.*

The childlike state is the manifestation of the works of the flesh.

Maturity is different from piety. Piety refers to the inner life of the Christian. Its visible manifestation is maturity. If we had to illustrate these 2 virtues, we could say that piety is the nature of the tree and that its fruit is maturity. We, therefore, have a responsibility to be accountable for our actions, to recognize them and to repent of them. We must not make another person bear the weight of our responsibility. We must not start condemning or accusing others as Adam did with Eve when they ate the forbidden fruit. Rather, we need to remove what is childish in us in order to manifest the adult dimension.

1 Corinthians 13:11 *"When I was a child, I spoke as a child, I understood as a child, I thought as a child; but when I became a man, I put away childish things."*

III. OTHER FORMS OF DEMONSTRATING MATURITY

The adult dimension is also measurable in the way we make decisions and make our choices, even if they are unpopular. Maturity is also demonstrated in the practice of loyalty by remaining steadfast in our commitments, even when things do not go our way. Through maturity, I do not only understand who I am, but also who others are, as well as the community of which I am only one element among many others.

Maturity could also be considered as wisdom, since it allows us to think before we act and not after. It is a form of anticipation that makes us wise men. We will thus, spare the lives of many and protect the community.

Our whole life as servants will be devoted to the development of our Christian character, which means, maturity as the manifestation of Christian values. We aim to be like Christ, the model par excellence, without however becoming Jesus.

These values are described in the Bible as being the "fruit of the Spirit", namely: love, peace, faithfulness, patience, justice, self-control and integrity. For God, character is more important than charisma. If we lack maturity despite possessing the charisma, we will not be able to accomplish our mission neither in the eyes of God nor in the eyes of men.

Another way to see maturity is as the tip of the iceberg. It is therefore your testimony, your reputation.

Ecclesiastes 7:1 *A good name is better than precious ointment, and the day of death than the day of one's birth; A good reputation is worth more than precious ointment.*

Let us take a moment of personal reflection on this subject by asking ourselves some questions:

- What do people see as fruit in my life?
- What do I produce?
- What effect do I leave behind?
- He who sows to the flesh will reap corruption. We can only give what we have received. So, what do we get?
- Are we really ready in the depths of our conscience to occupy positions of responsibility?
- Or, are we still childlike (INFANS), that person who is weak-willed and needs to be defended, the one for whom the adult must do things?

IV. ONCE A SERVANT, ALWAYS A SERVANT, HENCE THE IMPORTANCE OF DISCIPLINE

Let us keep in mind, that from the day we received Jesus Christ as Lord and Savior, we all, without exception, became servants of God for life. The awareness that we are servants for life will push us to want to improve who we are and what we do. A popular adage teaches us that "the best of us is ourselves while we are improving." Without comparing ourselves to anyone else, by also knowing that it is to God that we offer service.

1Corinthians 9:26-27 *"Therefore I run thus: not with uncertainty. Thus I fight: not as one who beats the air. 27 But I discipline my body and bring it into subjection, lest, when I have preached to others, I myself should become disqualified."*

Let us keep the same mentality as that of the Apostle Paul recorded in the book of 1 Corinthians. Even after we have been powerfully used by the Lord, or after having accomplished great things, let us say, as the biblical passage of Luke 17:10 says, "So likewise you, when you have done all those things which you are commanded, say, 'We are unprofitable servants. We have done what was our duty to do.'"

When we read the book of Joshua in chapter 12:31, we see him accomplishing great things. In chapter 13:1, the Lord asks him not to consider them, but to get back to the work.

The apostle Paul said, "I have fought the good fight, I have kept the faith." This mentality of staying focused until the end, reveals the kind of discipline the Apostle had developed, and this, despite the fact that he had experienced di cult moments in his walk.

2 Corinthians 11:23-28 *"Are they ministers of Christ?—I speak as a fool— I am more: in labors more abundant, in stripes above measure, in prisons more frequently, in deaths often. 24 From the Jews five times I received forty stripes minus one. 25 Three times I was beaten with rods; once I was stoned; three times I was shipwrecked; a night and a day I have been in the deep; 26 in journeys often, in perils of waters, in perils of robbers, in perils of my own countrymen, in perils of the Gentiles, in perils in the city, in perils in the wilderness, in perils in the sea, in perils among false brethren; 27 in weariness and toil, in sleeplessness often, in hunger and thirst, in fastings often, in cold and nakedness— 28 besides the other things, what comes upon me daily: my deep concern for all the churches."*

We must be interested in what is essential, rather than what is accessory, in what is useful and not pleasant, in what is important and not urgent, in what is priority and not secondary, and above all prefer character over charisma.

Charisma is irrevocable. It is given to every man by God. We do not have to make any e ort to develop it. Character, on the other hand, must be developed by man himself. It is man's offering to God, that is, the quality of life that we produce and that we o er to the Lord.

God is not so much interested in charisma, but rather, in character.

CONCLUSION

In a big house, there are several vases of different utility. Our approach is to become the vase of honor, useful to the Master. We must offer Him a service of quality, the service He really expects from us.

Being Good Servants
As we have repeated many times in this book, the Lord is really looking for good servants. He is looking for worshipers (servants) whom the Father asks for. These are the ones who will worship Him in spirit and in truth. The Lord is looking for workers who will do His will and not their own. It is this type of service that will trigger the manifestation of His power on this earth.

Proverbs 20:6 *Most men will proclaim each his own goodness, But who can find a faithful man?*

To explain this verse in other terms: people who proclaim their own goodness are those who perform several activities and different types of services in order to be well seen, according to their flesh. But, what about the service wanted and judged by the Lord, according to His standards?

The Lord Jesus Christ gave birth to the Church and recommends that we belong to a fixed congregation, a local church. We need to understand that our service is part of a collective spirit for the advancement of the Kingdom of God. The good servant serves God in his local church. Let us therefore not serve the Lord for our own personal interests, with wanting to achieve our own ambitions, or out of frivolity for our own pleasure. Let us serve the Lord with a spirit of commitment, and not by refusing the supervision of the Pastor, which is the order wanted by God for the accomplishment of the mission of His church. Let us also serve the Lord as men who have received recommendation and revelation from Him without expecting any rewards in return from men.

Let us not forget that every Christian is called to be a disciple. Let us therefore be stable disciples on whom the local assembly can count as loyal, trained and hardworking servants.

Beware of the trap of knowledge. We are not taught to be stingy with knowledge, but to allow others to access this knowledge as well. Our concern should be to always remain vases of honor for the Lord. Let us go and seek the lost souls so that they can experience salvation in Jesus Christ. Let us also see to it that these souls get the best guidance of the local church-sheepfold. It is our responsibility to speak well of the congregation to which we belong. Let us not forget that when we evangelize, our consistency in applying biblical principles is more effective than our words.

The service
While serving God, the heart of man is the most important element. Our first love for the Lord must not be turned o .

May it not be, as the book of Revelation says to the church of Ephesus, replaced by any other kind of love!

The church of Ephesus had love for the Lord, but had lost the first love! The reasons for this first love were healthy and allowed the Spirit to work unhindered. For a Christian, first love means that everything in him, and everything that he has, is for God. May we keep the flame of this love alive and the same motivation that we experienced at the beginning of our walk with the Lord! To do this, let us maintain our life of intimacy and listening every day, so that we never fall into routine, habits or tradition. It is first of all our being that must become an offering, a service for this great God. Even before consuming our talent, may the Lord take pleasure in consuming our life as a sweet-smelling offering.

Genesis 4:4 *Abel also brought of the firstborn of his flock and of their fat. And the Lord respected Abel and his offering,*

God first accepted Abel before his offering. It is first of all the man whom he approves of.

2Corinthians 8:5 *And not only as we had hoped, but they first gave themselves to the Lord, and then to us by the will of God.*

Man first gives himself to God, then, comes the service. Since the service we render to the Lord will have repercussions in eternity, we are advised to do it with fear and trembling, with love and excellence, far from murmurings and complaints.

The Bible recommends that everyone be careful of how they build. In other words, everyone should be careful of how they serve. If others build with hay, it is up to us to build with enduring spiritual materials. Let us build by wanting to sustain the work, so that future generations can bene t from it. This is the example of Jacob the patriarch.

The Samaritan woman who was talking to Jesus referred to the work of her ancestor, saying to Jesus "Are you greater than our father Jacob, who worked and who gave us the well?" The service we render to God is the testimony of our love, our humility and our consideration for His person. "What do you have that you have not received and if you have received it, why do you behave as if you have not received it? We owe God everything, but nothing. So let us avoid excuses, let us not choose as we please whom to serve, when to serve, why to serve, but let us give ourselves entirely to the Lord.

God is Spirit and needs us in order to materialize Himself. He wants to use our eyes, our hands, our talents and our feet to accomplish His work. Are we willing to do so?

1 Corinthians 15:58 *"Therefore, my beloved brethren, be steadfast, immovable, always abounding in the work of the Lord, knowing that your labor is not in vain in the Lord."*

1 Peter 2:9 *"But you are a chosen generation, a royal priesthood, a holy nation, His own special people, that you may proclaim the praises of Him who called you out of darkness into His marvelous light."*

Our Responsibility Towards our Local Assembly
The local church is the spiritual family intended by God for the growth of every Christian. Despite the abuses that may have occurred, it remains indispensable.

If there are abuses of authority in a biological family, we cannot conclude that the family is useless for any human being! The same is true for the church. Man must be traceable in the eyes of God and men. He must have a fixed pastor and a fixed church. His service must be supervised. He must be able to bene t from the care and guidance of a visible shepherd.

Hannah handed over her young son, Samuel, to the priest, Eli, to be consecrated in the temple for the service of God. Eli had to supervise Samuel in order to ensure the transmission of the sacred work. Without Eli transmitting his knowledge to Samuel, he never could have served as prophet, priest and judge. But, Hannah may have had good reason not to entrust Samuel to Eli. Eli's children had a very bad testimony. They behaved badly and had no fear of God at all. That said, Eli did not behave like them. The mistakes of men do not cancel applying God's established principles.

The local church is an embassy, the organization of God's service on earth. It was Jesus who said, "I will build My church and the gates of hell shall not prevail against it." Has this word of Christ become obsolete for us today? Has Jesus changed? Should the visible church no longer exist? Of course not. The words of Christ are still relevant. The local church must still exist and is important for every Christian regardless of his or her social rank.

What explanation will we give to God if we fail to fulfill our spiritual duties? Excuses and complaints will not change the will of the Lord. All those who serve the Lord with zeal and according to His will, have been and still are confronted with the same realities, the same oppositions, and experience the same victories by faith. Let us, therefore, commit ourselves and make this firm resolution to obey God. If some people do not want to serve Him seriously, let us at least be among the first ones to do so. Let us be fighters for Christ.

May our works emanate from the Master's will! Let us get closer to the Lord and become true ambassadors of His Kingdom by our way of serving Him. May the Lord be pleased to testify from heaven of our service, as a sweet-smelling offering, as He did for Job!

Job 1:8 *Then the Lord said to Satan, "Have you considered my servant Job, that there is none like him on the earth, a blameless and upright man, one who fears God and shuns evil?"*

In the book of Exodus, God promises those who serve Him to bless their water, their bread, to fight disease, barrenness and to prolong the days of their life on earth. With the Lord, the problem has never been the lack of oil to fill, but the absence of vases!

Let us, therefore, prepare ourselves to be vases that the Lord will continue to fill so that we may bring life, healing and well-being to people in the most effective way possible.

May the Lord bless His Church!

BIBLIOGRAPHY

A. Kuen. "Les lettres de Paul" [Paul's letters]Emmaüs Edition 1806 Saint-Légier - (Switzerland) 1982

D.H.Mills "Loyauté et déloyauté" [Loyalty and Disloyalty] Parchement House - 2017

W.Nee "le vrai serviteur de Dieu" [a true servant of God] IMEAF, 26160 France - 2008

D.H. Mills "Croissance de l'église " [A Church growth] Parchment House 2017

Dictionnaire Grec-Français du Nouveau Testament, société biblique française

J. Stott. "La lettre aux Éphésiens, Grâce et vérité" [A Letter to Ephesians, Grace and Truth], MulhouseFrance1995

A.Kuen. "Encyclopédie des questions" [Encyclopedia of Questions] Emmaüs - Edition 1806 Saint-Légier (Switzerland) 2020

BIOGRAPHY

Since 2002, Pastor Taty Okuan founded, and is the leading Pastor of the community of "Centre Évangélique de la Restauration," located in Ghent, Belgium. He is married to Emmanuelle Muleka and is the father of four daughters – Rachel, Tatiana, Kérène and Marie Rose.

Immediately after obtaining his State degree, he completed his studies in Interior Architecture in Zaire (now Democratic Republic of the Congo). He then obtained a degree in Biblical Studies at the Rhema Bible Training Center in Johannesburg, South Africa. He also took theology courses at the Continental Theological Seminary in Belgium. He holds a degree in practical psychology, child psychology and marriage counseling.

Pastor Taty is a preacher, a trainer, a teacher, a speaker, a versatile counselor and de fines himself as a motivator, who has received a powerful message of soul restoration from the Lord.

Passionate about the cause of Jesus Christ, and a fervent defender of Christian doctrine, he has helped many people discover their callings, both in the ecclesiastical and secular fields.

Serving God in the local church

ABOUT THE BOOK

God did not create man to live alone. For the born again believer, the church of God is, and always will be the family established by God to ensure our spiritual growth to the fullest. Despite the abuses that may have occurred, it remains indispensable. Therefore, every Christian should belong to a local church, a unit of the universal Church, and be traceable by God and men.

Yet still, questions like, "is serving God in a local church still necessary? Can I not serve God from the isolation of my home?" are been asked or have asked either innocently or in the face of several factors that have tainted the image of the church. This book propagates not only the importance and significance of serving in our local church, but also how, as plainly as it can be understood based on the word of God.

For we are saved to serve! Read and be blessedly inspired to serve God in the family of God.

ABOUT THE AUTHOR

Pastor Taty Okuan is the founder and head pastor of the Centre Evangelique de la Restauration (Evangelical Centre of Restauration) in Belgium.

Preacher, trainer, speaker, counselor, he defines himself as a motivator having received from the Lord a powerful message of soul restauration.

ISBN 9789464753691

9789464753691

9789464753691

Book designer: BubscriptServices

Gsm +32 499 901 865

Printed in the United States
by Baker & Taylor Publisher Services